HOMELAND SECURITY AND THE NEED FOR CHANGE

Organizing Principles,
Governing Institutions,
and American Culture

HOMELAND SECURITY AND THE NEED FOR CHANGE

Organizing Principles, Governing Institutions, and American Culture

Michael J. Hillyard

Published by Aventine Press, LLC
45 East Flower Street, Ste. 236
Chula Vista, CA 91910-7631, USA

www.aventinepress.com

ISBN: 1-59330-012-3

Printed in the United States of America

TABLE OF CONTENTS

I am certainly not an advocate for frequent changes in laws and constitutions. I think moderate imperfections had better be borne with; because, when once known, we accommodate ourselves to them, and find practical means of correcting their ill effect. But I know also, that laws and institutions must go hand in hand with the progress of the human mind. As that becomes more developed, more enlightened, as new discoveries are made, new truths discovered and manners and opinions change, with the change of circumstances, institutions must advance also to keep pace with the times. We might as well require a man to wear still the coat which fitted him when a boy as civilized society to remain ever under the regimen of their barbarous ancestors.[1]

- Thomas Jefferson in a July 12, 1816 letter to Samuel Kercheval

PREFACE

The decision to write a book on homeland security was made in the wake of September 11, when I watched and re-watched video of the planes crashing into the World Trade Center and all of the tragic consequences those planes wrought. I thought again and again about how I might contribute to the war on terrorism. Having served in the U.S. military, led a higher education institution, and conducted significant research in public crisis management and citizen service, I thought my greatest contribution would be to spend a full year of my free time thinking, researching, and writing to assist the nation's homeland security cause. I did not want to restrict myself to hard evidence, scholarly opinion, or practical insight. I just sought to uncover relevant issues. I was looking for anything related to homeland security that might not have been considered, or any angle that might not have been taken by the many government, non-governmental, academic, and other dedicated professionals who were doing all they could to come up with answers to the problems that plague our governments and people.

Throughout my work I recognized a theme for today's rapidly evolving homeland security situation that Jeff Shaara captured in his *Rise to Rebellion* novel of the American Revolution generation. We as a nation are having an at-large conversation similar to one between George Washington and Ben Franklin upon Washington's being voted Commander of the Continental Army by the Second Continental Congress.

Washington said to Franklin, "Doctor, I am not so sure about this. I am afraid that I am but an amateur in these affairs."

Franklin put a hand on his shoulder, and (John) Adams heard the old man say with a laugh, "So are we all, Colonel. So are we all."

Since this book purposely raises issues that have either been absent from or tangential to the core discussions of homeland security, it is by no means intended to be a comprehensive study. Those who attempt to read it as such will find it both disjointed and incomplete. Its intended value is in the individual conceptual issues its essays raise. If taken together, they might (hopefully) combine with other ideas to form the framework for a system of homeland security. The book can and should be read in its various pieces - the individual essays that comprise each of the different chapters - and as a whole, so long as the reader reflects on the rest of the burgeoning body of homeland security knowledge - the many journal articles, conferences, commissions, congressional hearings, and executive department papers. Regardless of how the book is read, one should not expect to find all of the answers (or even all of the questions) here.

This book's seven essays focus on three general topics:

(1) Describing an organization for homeland security by articulating the organizational principles behind such organization.
(2) Defining homeland security roles for key public and other institutions that have yet to be considered, and what including such institutions reveals about which people and organizations are ultimately responsible for national security. Two institutions are covered in

detail but similar essays could be written about other institutions' roles in this major public priority.

(3) Identifying a homeland security role for citizens as the first litmus test of a twenty-first century democratic republic. Homeland security dialogue is currently focused on what government is and is not doing; citizens have a homeland security burden to bear that is directly tied to their citizenship.

The research methods behind the essays reflect its interdisciplinary subject. History, management science, social sciences, and case studies are all applied herein.

My greatest hope for this book is that someone, somewhere uses the information as an idea or set of ideas that might be implemented, strengthens his or her understanding of the homeland security imperative, counterbalances contrary views or conventional wisdom, or triggers another thought that merges the reader's understanding of homeland security with what is provided here. No matter how the book is received and subsequently acted on (if at all), if its contents are somehow translated into the homeland security cause, then it will have been worth the effort.

Michael J. Hillyard
January 12, 2003

CHAPTER ONE

WHAT ABOUT YOUR BLOCK?
A NEW FEDERAL DEPARTMENT
IS MUCH NEEDED...
BUT THE FIGHT AGAINST
TERROR BEGINS LOCALLY

Introduction

The United States is at war on its homeland. In the face of a common enemy, this war will either challenge American society to form a more perfect union in line with its ideals, or it will weaken that society through cultural inattention and a political/governance framework that together permits cancerous enemies to first lodge and grow within its presence and then exploit the gaps and inefficiencies in its federalist system to bring a republic to its knees. The greatest question of this century is:

Will America be viewed as the democratic republican example that allowed and enabled the realization of freedoms inherent in its stated ideals as they are embodied in the Declaration of Independence and the Constitution of the United States, or will this generation have failed to adapt under Thomas Jefferson's belief that each generation must rethink its "laws and institutions...hand in hand with the progress of the human mind."

The enemies to liberty, freedom, and capitalism have most certainly progressed; their progress is evidenced in the destruction wrought both in the United States and abroad. Will the United States similarly shed, as Jefferson said, "the coat" of its ancestors - the contemporary American culture and institutions that are being exploited? It can, it should, and it must.

A version of the essay below was first published as an editorial in Newsday.[2]

Legislation that created the Department of Homeland Security is a first step to a more secure homeland. But the attention being paid to it - we keep hearing how this is the largest government reorganization in 50 years - is distorting how much the federal government can achieve against terrorism and provides false assurance that we are taking the most appropriate steps to secure our country.

Homeland security starts not with the federal government but at the local level, where citizens, police and emergency services, and government are woefully unprepared for a terrorist attack. This problem stems as much from the dismissal of September 11 as a one-time aberration as it does from a lack of time and resources. The urgency of the situation was described in the title of a recent report sponsored by the Council on Foreign Relations: "America Still Unprepared - America Still in Danger."

Localizing homeland security needs to become the nation's number-one objective. In doing so, we follow the reasoning of James Madison in Federalist Paper No. 41: "The means of security can only be regulated by the means and danger of attack."

In the case of terrorism on U.S. soil, the attack is carried out by dispersed individuals, some of whom use our civil liberties to hide among us and blend in

as citizens. They employ their own resources in combination with ours - hijacked airliners for example - to
create weapons. The danger is to individual citizens
and groups of citizens in specific locations - most likely
in large population centers, or near famous monuments
or other symbols of American power.

With the means and danger of attack both locally
based, security is best regulated through a focus on
the citizen and the community. Instead of becoming
a stealthy enemy's passive target, the citizen and the
community must become the primary participants in
creating security. As in Israel, which has suffered terrorist attacks for years, permanent citizen mobilization
must become a way of life.

Local government is the only institution capable of
providing a framework for millions of citizens to gather
and report information, receive emergency supplies,
engage in pre-crisis planning, and practice mobilization,
evacuation, response and recovery operations. Against
a threat from a conventional military nation-state, where
the danger came from overseas, federal institutions
were necessarily predominant.

But at home against terrorists, these institutions
are best used as a support system. We need to fight
terrorism much the way we fight wildland fires. A
cooperative of seven federal agencies and 50 state organizations together decide national wildfire policy
and set common standards and training, assuring inter-
changeable assets and equipment. But fires are fought
by local firefighters who call in federal or out-of-state
help only if they become overwhelmed and depleted.

Another model is the nation's emergency management system. The State of Delaware, for example,
maintains county emergency management offices, a
state-level emergency management agency that arranges

support for counties that request it and 19 interstate compacts for inter-state support. Federal support is available through the Federal Emergency Management Agency's office in Philadelphia.

If reliance on citizens under voluntary and local authority seems the polar opposite of this past century's national security dependency on professionals under federal authority, it is. While citizens have generously served this nation's national security interests abroad in direct federal service as GIs or intelligence professionals or at home in war production, we have not regularly and systematically engaged the enemy from our front porch, community center or marketplace, as we must now.

There is a precedent for such involvement. During the American Revolution, this land was similarly the battleground for a protracted engagement, our domestic way of life swung in the balance, an enemy of both foreign and domestic composition - Tory colonists, the British Army and foreign mercenaries - fought against us and the danger of attack was focused specifically on citizens and their property.

Homeland security is as much a litmus test of the citizen's role in a 21st-century democracy as the Battle of Lexington and Concord was for the 18th-century colonists who took the fight from their homes to Boston's surrounding countryside and put the British on notice. Our Lexington and Concord starts by renewing our pledge to our communities, meeting our neighbors and working together to make America a place where terrorists cannot hide.

In neighborhoods of strangers, anyone can function as a threat without being noticed. We must assume the responsibility of watching for and reporting information, preparing our homes, attending planning sessions and taking a periodic day off of work to practice a homeland security simulation.

President George W. Bush's Terrorist Information and Prevention System proposal, whereby small groups of transportation, maritime and other industry personnel would report unusual activity, was a step in this direction. Civil liberties concerns about spying on one's neighbor killed the initiative but we need to address those concerns and create a citizen-reporting system. Non-security institutions must also be empowered as information sources. For example, the U.S. Postal Service visits every house and business daily. If trained in basic information gathering and handheld computer data-entry, letter carriers could make a big contribution to security.

At the same time, local government must evolve its agencies and infrastructure. Specialists could facilitate the coordination of public functions, such as police, fire, emergency medical service and public health, and help citizens develop plans for community intelligence gathering, response, and recovery.

Co-chairs of the U.S. Commission on National Security, Gary Hart and Warren Rudman report that local "public health departments are barely funded...medical professionals often lack the training to diagnose and treat diseases...reporting systems are antiquated, slow, and outmoded." No function needs more improvement in our national security strategy.

State and federal institutions also need to evolve. The National Guard, for example, is a logical state-level force-in-readiness. Right now, it is still primarily focused for roles overseas in support of U.S. forces.

Federal reorganization is just one step to homeland security. Even as he lobbied hard for the new agency,

President Bush acknowledged the roles of both citizen and local government. He knows we need to "rally our entire society," with "individual volunteers... channel[ing] their energy and commitment." He wonders, "What should non-federal governments, the private sector, and citizens do to help secure the homeland?"

Certainly we must rally at the local level. But as the Homeland Security agency gets under way, we also must ask what the federal government can do to help us. The entire nation must see homeland security for the house-to-house, neighbor-to-neighbor, community-to-community issue it is; otherwise, we are in for a very long century.

CHAPTER TWO

HOMELAND SECURITY'S
ORGANIZING PRINCIPLES

A version of this essay appeared in the U.S. Army War College Quarterly, *Parameters*.[3]

Capsule Summary

President George W. Bush's creations of the Office of Homeland Security, Homeland Security Council, and Department of Homeland Security are first steps to institutionalizing homeland security both at the federal level in a standing bureaucracy and as a national network to draw upon all national resources. A hybrid institution that combines both federal and national power in bureaucracy and network form could provide a principles-based, enduring homeland security structure. The bureaucratic organizational aspects of such an institution will provide homeland security functions that are purely federal in scope under the aegis of the federal department. The federal department should then serve as an important nucleus for an expansive national homeland security network among other national resources, to include the vast panoply of regional, state, local, and community organizations and individuals associated with securing the homeland and its people.

Defining the Homeland Security Question

In their bestselling 1994 business text, *Built to Last: Successful Habits of Visionary Companies*, Professors James Collins and Jerry Porras identify common principles at the heart of the world's premier lasting corporations.[4] Similarly, in *Bureaucracy: What Government Agencies Do and Why They Do It*,[5] renowned public policy expert James Wilson identifies the principles shared by leading public organizations. Common among both corporate and government successes is a focus foremost on the institution and only secondarily on the specific mission, product, or service provided by the institution. The message these organizations send is: *while missions, products, and services may change, institutions endure.* Another common theme is people; specifically, people matter in leading institutions. What people believe as core ideologies generation after generation uphold and advance the organization as an institution. Second tier organizations, both public and private, focus on issues other than the institution - a specific mission to perform, a key product to deliver, a special service to render, a target profit to make. With ideology affixed to other factors and not the institution, a change in any of the factors sends shock waves through the institution, and over the long haul, substantial change leads to instability, if not chaos.

The distinction between institution as what endures, and mission, product, or service as what may someday change, is important as the nation addresses its structure for homeland security. Contemporary missions - border security; coastal protection; counterterrorism; biological, chemical, and nuclear defense; emergency management; among the many others - dominate the focus of current policy discussions. How do we defend against this?

How do we prepare for that? How do we respond to x? How do we recover from y? In the wake of a national crisis, the immediate threats rightfully take center stage over discussions of long term institutional design. But, when the national discussion of homeland security starts with specific threats for which the nation is unprepared, answers that produce long term institutional consequences quite naturally follow. Unfortunately, in first asking the specific questions, and then searching for their subsequent answers, the institutional principle of successful organizations is violated. Answers of czars, realignments of bureaucracies, creation of new bureaucracies, and facilitation of existing federal, state, local, and non-governmental organizations address the immediate. When framed as answers for threats against which the nation has no coherent response, all such answers hold a certain logic. But, all such answers logically solve the wrong question.

Just as leading organizations do, both the federal and national organization for homeland security must provide an enduring answer to a question that most Americans know will never go away, and that is:

How can the security of the United States people and their way of life be institutionalized through national capabilities to mitigate, prepare for, respond to, recover from, and learn from threats known and unknown?

If this question is answered with the appropriate institutional response, then the nation can rest assured that its homeland security apparatus will be enduring and effective. Reflecting the enormity of the homeland security challenge, the question itself lacks focus, and justifiably so. The answer's *breadth* currently spans a wide variety of contemporary *targets* to include geography at home and abroad, technology, national symbols, and people; *human response resources*, to include federal, regional, state, and local authorities, non-profit and voluntary organizations, businesses, specialists, and citizens; *functional assets*, to include legal, intelligence, safety, law enforcement, public health, among others; and *threats*, to include foreign and domestic terrorist groups and individuals, foreign conventional powers, rogue regimes, mother nature, disease, and technological disaster. The answer's *depth* spans the international organization and coalition down to the individual citizen. But, the vastness of the difficult question paradoxically provides an opportunity to arrive at the appropriately enduring institutional response. Just as leading organizations have difficulty in pinning down a timelessly precise organizational product, service, or mission, so will a lasting homeland institution have difficulty in addressing a timelessly specific threat for which it is meant to exist, with a key difference being that the homeland security institutional history has yet to be written.

The Federal Homeland Security Institution

President Bush's establishment of an Office of Homeland Security was an important first step towards what should become an evolving federal institution. As stated in the White House Press Release that introduced the office:

The mission of the Office will be to develop and coordinate the implementation of a comprehensive national strategy to secure the United States from terrorist threats or attacks. The Office will coordinate the executive branch's efforts to detect, prepare for, prevent,

protect against, respond to, and recover from terrorist
attacks within the United States.[6]

The Office of Homeland Security, initially headed
by former Pennsylvania Governor Tom Ridge as the
Assistant to the President for Homeland Security, was
specifically responsible for coordination of national
strategy, detection, preparedness, prevention, protection,
response, recovery, incident management, continuity
of government, public affairs, legal issues, budgets,
and administration associated with the government's
terrorism efforts.[7] As a first step towards homeland
security institutionalization, President Bush established the idea that a standing federal office designed
for homeland security is critically important to coordinate and facilitate the many resources at the nation's
disposal. As a federal institution that will serve the
Nation throughout the 21st Century, the office needed
to and eventually did evolve from its origin as a small
coordination staff with responsibility for terrorism-
focused facilitation and coordination of all federal
departments and agencies, state and local governments,
and private industry into a true federal bureaucracy
(i.e.: the Department of Homeland Security) that spans
the homeland security spectrum.

Accepting the notion that building a homeland security institution is more advantageous than aligning
something short of an institution to counter contemporary threats, the first portion of the answer to the
homeland security question is a federal one. Addressed
before Congress by former Senator Gary Hart, co-chair
of the Commission for U.S. National Security/21st
Century, Hart rightfully asked first how the nation
might institutionalize the security of the homeland
and only then identifies the federal government as a

primary foundation for such institutionalization. His question importantly leads to an expansive definition of homeland security to extend beyond international terrorism to incorporate other threats to the American people, which include natural, human, and techno-logical disasters. The linkage is appropriate because so many federal, state, and local systems must addresses the same response issues for multiple purposes. In just one example among countless numbers of others around the country, the Washington, D.C. transportation system is structurally corked by several strategic choke points that currently prevent a timely citizen emergency exodus. Such an exodus could be required for a host of different reasons, only one reason for such action is international terrorism. Federal organization needs to be aligned where threats to the homeland logically in-tersect.

While Governor Ridge's close working relationship with President Bush initially assured the coordination and facilitation expected by the President on a major homeland security issue - terrorism - it became critically important to institutionalize a federal bureaucracy for the long term out of the many disparate departments and agencies that play roles in homeland security. Although Ridge (and implicitly, the President) said he would have "all the resources I need," some members of the admin-istration knew that even Ridge's relationship and clout were not enough to realign priorities and missions on even just the limited terrorism issue, with one official stating that the new office was "set up for failure."[8]

A lasting federal organization must oversee current federal homeland security missions and anticipate future missions. Such missions include but are not limited to protection of the many different points of entry into the United States, intracontinental and intercontinental transportation, emergency and disaster management, and technological security, among others. But as stated earlier, such missions will change over time. What the federal institution for homeland security must provide is continuity of homeland security purpose on issues of overarching policy, legislation, and executive action as missions change, evolve, and emerge around this dynamic issue. The key institutional principle to be assured is the need to maintain a standing federal organization that accepts as its charter, whose leadership takes on its shoulders, and whose people adopt as their core ideology, the security of the American homeland. Without a standing, centralizing, galvanizing focus in the federal government, there can be no enduring homeland security institution. Such a focus is created through a federal department that possesses capabilities to align, coordinate, and reallocate people and resources to priority federal missions; create a bureaucratic culture around homeland security complete with a generation of civil servants aligned with its core ideology; argue for and implement federal policy; coordinate with other federal departments as an equal; and facilitate the national network (to be described below) as its nucleus. It is precisely this federal mandate that the new Department of Homeland Security must assume as an organization and the Secretary of Homeland Security must embody as its leader.

Beyond Organizational Behavior: The National Homeland Security Institution

Where the paths of homeland security and organizational behavior veer is in the sheer enormity posed of the homeland security challenge. The nature of the task - security of the homeland - with its many considerations - size, scale, skills, scope, breadth, depth - necessitates an interorganizational structure. It is impossible to conceive of homeland security being conducted solely by a single organization, even by an hypothesized domestic bureaucracy the size and scale of the Department of Defense. There is simply too much expertise to be garnered, too much potential for redundancy. Conversely, even with the addition of the Department of Homeland Security, it is still difficult to imagine a cohesive national homeland security process emerging out of the chaotic coordination that currently exists between and among federal, state, and local departments and agencies. When state governors, such as Idaho's Dirk Kempthorne, report that his National Guard adjutant-general is not permitted to share certain information with him,[9] it is clear that a deep institutional problem exists, and that the problem is at least in part a federal one. When a local cop wonders why he might need to check for flight manuals as well as drugs in the speeding vehicles he pulls over,[10] it is clear that this problem, while national in scope, is also very much local in implementation. A federally focused institution for national homeland security is not the complete answer.

While discussions of the federal role easily formed into dialogue and debate which led to the federal department's legislation, even its proponents seem to miss the second and equally important foundation of what could evolve as a truly *national* homeland security institution. *The Advisory Panel to Assess Domestic Response Capabilities for Terrorism Involving Weapons of Mass Destruction* (hereafter referred to as the Gilmore Commission) recognized the lack of attention paid to state and local levels:

...we need a national approach, one that recognizes the unique individual skills that communities, states, and the federal government possess that, collectively, will give us the "total package" needed to address all aspects of terrorism.[11]

As argued for in the Gilmore Commission on its narrowly chartered issue of terrorism, the creation of the Department of Homeland Security lays the groundwork for a more comprehensive national institution across the range of homeland security issues, in which the federal government will play only one of the many necessary national roles. When considering the national structure of homeland security, that structure must incorporate the many functional, jurisdictionary, and constituency boundaries that the threats cross. The structure must leverage, not conflict with, the many boundaries it crosses and peoples it serves. The paradox that must be realized in the homeland security answer is the crossing of boundaries to leverage the capabilities of the very boundaries that are crossed. Functional boundaries include fire, police, legal, public health, military, aviation, among others. Jurisdictional boundaries include international, federal, state, and local levels. Constituencies include a variety of professional communities, corporations, and what is potentially homeland security's greatest weapon - the American citizen. At the very heart of the national institution for homeland security must be the citizen as both the reason for the institution as well as the institution's greatest asset in the form of the citizen-servant. With the citizen at the heart of the institution, the need for organizational structure close to the citizen is imperative. As evidenced in the Federal Civil Defense Administration's failure to internalize civil defense in the American mind, a federal bureaucracy will never capably mobilize and manage the information and resources necessary to leverage tens of millions of American first responders and everyday citizens as part of the enduring solution for homeland security.

The only structure capable of shaping jurisdictions, levels, functions, and leaders, managers, experts, first responders, and citizens into a national homeland security institution is an interorganizational crisis response network. By their very nature, interorganizational crisis response networks possess principles in multi-organizational form similar to those of enduring singular organizations. The principles, like those of their organizational counterparts, are timeless and inviolable. They include common network purposes, a single authority structure, incentives for member organizations, a network macroculture, and an interoperable interorganizational structure.[12] Adoption of these principles in a national homeland security network will provide the second part of America's homeland security hybrid institution.

Common Purposes

Interorganizational crisis response networks possess fundamental reasons for otherwise disparate organizations to commonly work together. Organizations that form a network arrangement to assume collective responsibilities recognize, support, and approve of the overall purposes for their coming together. Without agreement on such purposes, or if such purposes are imposed on member organizations by an external authority (such as the federal government), a crisis response network will not optimally function. An example of a highly effective public crisis network is one facilitated through the National Interagency Fire Center (NIFC), in which seven federal agencies, 50 state organizations, and associated organizations commonly agree to overarching missions and prioritization of resources associated with the preparation, response, and recovery for and from wildland fires. Networks such as the one coordinated through the NIFC also possess a common understanding of the divisions of organizational labor that support the collective responsibilities. In the NIFC-facilitated network, each member organization understands its role and the roles of other member organizations in support of the wildland fire institution. Each organization also retains its organizational autonomy and separate missions outside of the network; and it is the uniqueness of each organization as it is brought to bear among the other network organizations that creates exponentially beneficial results when the network functions collectively.

A network for homeland security would provide an opportunity for organizations at its many different levels and from among its many different functions to address the overarching purposes, roles, and missions associated with their collective responsibility to secure the homeland. Importantly, the federal homeland security department would sit as only one member (albeit a dominant member that would ensure federal policy was implemented, federal monies were spent in accordance with their intended purposes, and other federal departments and agencies were aligned to support network needs) of the many different member organizations at the proverbial table.

At the strategic level, President Bush has created an initial structure that provides for the type of interorganizational arrangement that can lead to long-term network success. In his homeland security executive order, the

President provides for a Homeland Security Council that will "serve as the mechanism for ensuring coordination of homeland security-related activities of executive departments and agencies and effective development of homeland security policies."[13] Federal membership includes the parties who possess the authority to speak for the overarching leadership (i.e.: President and Vice-President), respective federal functions (i.e.: Secretary of the Treasury, Secretary of Defense, Attorney General, Secretary of Health and Human Services, Secretary of Transportation, Director of FEMA, Director of FBI, Director of CIA), and interorganizational coordination, facilitation, strategy, and action (i.e.: Assistant to the President for Homeland Security).[14] As is witnessed in other successful networks, the Homeland Security Council provides member organizations with necessary strategic representation to maintain the purposes of the network and coordinate individual organizational roles and responsibilities. The President should consider adding a state governor, county commissioner, and metropolitan mayor to ensure strategic representation of state and local interests. Also critically important is the President's directive to provide augmentation by other senior leaders from his cabinet when their services are deemed necessary.

Evolving to mirror the President's steps at the strategic level, the national institution will need to develop an operational element at the federal level to ensure the Council's intent is followed, and it will also need to develop regional and/or state level networks to mirror the components of the strategic level. The network's common purposes must be realized through all of the levels on which the network will function, which in the case of homeland security, is down to the organizations that support individual citizens and first responders.

Authority

Interorganizational network authority is secure in two forms: operational control and resource allocation. Organizations within a network defer to the network-identified authority in both of these distinct forms of authority. The most pervasive example of operational control is visible in the Incident Command System, which is used in many different crisis management communities. Based on the situation at hand, the network assigns appropriate command and control responsibilities at either operational or tactical levels. In the event of scare resources, resource prioritization, allocation, and distribution is also centralized in the network, with member organizations willingly submitting individual organizational participation to network authority. As indicated by retired General Barry McCaffrey in just one area of homeland security, there is no hint of such a principle being realized in border security:

> *At each point of entry on each sector - of our land border, and in every maritime approach - there is no single federal officer in charge.*[15]

The new Department of Homeland Security should produce the clear authority that is needed in border and all other homeland security.

A homeland security network could ensure network operational control through several different means, one being the establishment of a national operational council or operational commander whereby member organizations are either represented to reach consensus on prioritization and resource allocation, or they submit to a single, shared authority. This authority structure

would then be mimicked at regional and local levels
to ensure operational responsibility and autonomy to
problem solve at every stage in the network.

Included at the operational level, resource allocation
would be controlled through the operational authority,
but it would be achieved through the evolution of
a standard network infrastructure at each level, to
include identification and catalogue of all resources
(i.e.: people, equipment, supplies, volunteers, business
support, experts, etc.) at network disposal, thereby
enabling the rapid transition of resources from low to
high need areas. Both operational control and resource
allocation would be facilitated through the network
council's establishment of operational standards based
on the type, breadth, and depth of the homeland security
issue being faced, or the equipment used, or the training
required, or whatever else is needed.

Incentives

Networks provide member organizations with the
appropriate incentives to join and maintain membership
in the network, and such incentives extend well beyond
legislative enforcement to participate. Member organizations tend to *want* to avail the network of their
respective organizational services. Such an atmosphere
is created through incentives such as goodwill, reciprocation agreements, shared training and education
experiences, mutual response assurances, and network
budget allocations for services. Federal domination of
a homeland security network will not produce the types
of incentives necessary to induce willing participation
among other levels and functions of government or
non-government organizations. Federal participation

should exist alongside other member organizations to reach mutually beneficial solutions.

An ideal homeland security incentive structure would combine overarching federal policy and subsequent monetary and other resources with common sense on-the-ground realities provided through local, state, and functional member representatives. Federal monies would flow through the network in exchange for participation in communizing resources and ensuring the other incentives (e.g.: mutual response, submitting to network authority, etc.) listed above.

Macroculture

Networks take on cultural characteristics that extend beyond the member organizations' singular cultures. The homeland security network should take on a distinct cultural identity separate from both the federal homeland security institution and the other member organizations such as fire, police, emergency medical, emergency management, and public health. Central factors to network culture include: a core ideology, shared training and education, common symbols and experiences, and common language, among others. Critical to building a network macroculture in homeland security would be its extension to leaders, first responders, and citizens all over the country. The network would assume responsibility for the development of doctrine, standards, education, and training for all constituencies involved in homeland security down to the individual citizen, the nine million first responders that must be commonly prepared to face homeland security threats, mid-level managers from a wide range of functions, and senior leaders from private and public sectors.

The types of training in other networks that could apply to homeland security include a wide range of distance education, certification, seminars, wargames, simulations, and scenarios. A culture of homeland security will be realized when every police captain, fire and rescue employee, emergency medical technician, country emergency management director, port authority clerk, regional airport security chief, and county commissioner can personally identify his or her role in the nation's homeland security. Recognizing the need to infuse a pervasive national culture that reaches down to the lowest levels in the effort, the Gilmore Commission called for national strategy that would include homeland security training and education opportunities aimed at state and local response officials.[16]

Interorganizational Structure

Networks possess clearly defined structures, to include definitions and agreement on what organization fits where, common communications standards, reporting procedures, and intelligence dissemination both up and down the network chain. The structure enables the rapid movement of resources, information sharing, and mobilization of organizations and people to support network causes. The structure is typically provided for at the strategic level for mutual establishment of network purposes and priorities, at the operational level for the delivery of those purposes and priorities through decision making and movement of national resources, and at the tactical level through operational command and control. Critical to both the vertical and horizontal features of network facilitation are linking pins - individuals who have grown up in the network and possess operational knowledge beyond a single organization expertise. General McCaffrey identifies the current homeland shortfall when measured against the structural principle:

> *There is no common organizing scheme to the many federal agencies that are charged with these missions; no integrated intelligence or communications network; no common multiagency infrastructure development plan.*[17]

A properly structured homeland security network, integrated across the whole of America, has the potential to properly prepare and then rapidly mobilize both professionals and citizens in support of one or many homeland security crises at a single point in time. At the operational level, regional network hubs would coordinate national priorities in their region, establish the communications system for organizations in that region, maintain the skills, supplies, and equipment inventories, and provide for regional awareness of how and when organizations and individuals should plug into the network. From the regional level, local level hubs could provide the same duties at the level closest to most first responders and citizens. At every level the hubs would incorporate the Gilmore Commission's recommendation for functional representation of at least domestic preparedness; intelligence; health and medical; research, development, test, evaluation, and national standards; and management and budget.[18] Since the metropolitan public safety and regional emergency management communities would be member organizations in the homeland security network, physical infrastructure already exists as a foundation for the interorganizational structure.[19]

The Time Is Now

History and conventional wisdom conspire to create
a perception that institutional structures, particularly
when dealing with the federal government, take years or
even decades to evolve. As the crisis of September 11
illustrates, though, times have indeed changed. Terror
has the potential to strike quickly, close to home, at
any time, and in any place. Unfortunately, so do many
other threats to the homeland and its people, with both
terrorist and non-terrorist threats sharing many national
response resources. While homeland security as an
enduring institution may take years to mature, there
is no excuse to delay the difficult thinking, planning,
and political decision making associated with laying its
enduring foundation beyond just a federal Department
of Homeland Security. The citizenry should not have
to suffer through a bizarre configuration of temporary
arrangements before being provided with an institution
for their security in which they will play a leading role.
The time for change is now.

A Federal Bureaucracy and National Network

-Federal homeland security functions
-Focal point for federal policy
-Legislative liaison with Congress
-Coordination with other federal departments and agencies
-Federal role as nucleus for national homeland security institution
-Produces a generation of federal homeland security civil servants

<u>Membership</u> <u>Advisory</u>
  Federal   Science
  Regional   Technology
  State   Intelligence
  Local   Military
            Corporate

Department of Homeland Security
(Federal institution)
(Federal bureaucracy)

Federal homeland security roles & responsibilities

-Federal, state, & local coordination
-Functional alignment
-Response reciprocation
-Prioritization
-Resource allocation
-First responder training
-Citizen education
-Ensure common standards
-National Operational Authority
-Regional and local homeland security infrastructure

Homeland Security Council
(National institution)
(Interorganizational network)
(Strategic and operational levels)

America's homeland security network hub

Local Network Hubs
(Uses public safety Infrastructure)

Regional Network Hubs
(Uses emergency management infrastructure)

-Implementation and coordination down to first responder and citizen levels

CHAPTER THREE

HOMELAND SECURITY CULTURE

A version of this essay appeared in Belmont Publishing's *21st Century Defense: U.S. Joint Command.*[20]

"There is no need to suppose that human beings differ very much one from the other: but it is true that the ones who come out on top are the ones who have been trained in the hardest school."[21]

- Thucydides

Since implementation of the Goldwater-Nichols Department of Defense Reorganization Act of 1986, the military legacy is one of collective accomplishment in the pursuit and protection of national interests and security. Goldwater-Nichols effectively pulled together a previously independent set of military services - Army, Navy, Air Force, and Marine Corps - into a coordinated expression of national military power. All elements of military power have since been brought to bear in major and lesser contingencies, most recently in Afghanistan. Military success reflects a single-minded joint focus. Looking beyond the military, its unified command system and supporting joint architecture are unparalleled. In overcoming bureaucratic obstacles that afflict any group of organizations that recognize and commonly work towards common goals, today's joint military policy, doctrine, and operations provide an administrative model that other public organizations should replicate. And, the nation must consider the model's application to non-military national security interests.

In the September 11 aftermath, homeland security is the primary national concern. The military plays an important homeland security role. But, unlike in warfighting, it does not have the freedom of action among its own organizations to prescribe roles and missions under a unified commander and externally coordinate the joint effort with other organizations. In the homeland security equation the military is cast in a support role of other elements of national power. While the military role may be support and not primacy of operational purpose, and inherent differences are recognized between a multi-agency/multi-level homeland security organizational effort and an inter-military system, the principles of joint warfare translate for homeland security - they are just applied differently. If joint homeland security power is realized and appropriately harnessed, its potential size and scale will dwarf even the coordination, command, and control of resources in Afghanistan. And unlike a war, mobilization for homeland security never ends.

Homeland Security Public Law and Policy

Political decisions precede a system of joint national homeland security power. Questions similar to those asked and answered in Goldwater-Nichols must again be discussed. The discussion must lead to necessary answers in homeland security organization that will ultimately produce institutional alignment and reporting relationships among a number of levels and functions. Organization is the first step towards homefront effectiveness. At this level of policy, the chairman of the Advisory Panel to Assess Domestic Response Capabilities for Terrorism Involving Weapons of Mass Destruction (hereinafter referred to as the Gilmore Commission), former Governor of Virginia James Gilmore admits, "our most imposing challenge centers on policy and whether we have the collective fortitude to forge change, both in organization as well as process."[22] Gilmore's concern was voiced before September 11, and in its aftermath, the political decision making process has since been galvanized, similar to the causes and effects of Pearl Harbor and World War II that preceded passage of the National Security Act of 1947, and the Iran hostage rescue failure and invasion of Grenada that served as joint military legislation impetuses. The healthy political debate is unfolding on an expedient post-crisis course and (confidently speaking) it will produce a national homeland security structure.[23] That structure must include functional alignment, such as fire, police, emergency medical services, public health, public works, border and coastal patrol, information security, legal, military, among others; it must incorporate the many levels of government and non-government actors, to include international, federal, regional, state, local, and private; and it must integrate the many different types of expertise, to include elements of coordination, command, leadership, support, intelligence, science, and logistics, among others.

The structure must result in organizational design that replicates those principles inherent in the joint military system that extend beyond the battlefield to the homefront. Such principles apply at a general level whenever a group of disparate crisis-oriented organizations gather for sustained, collective goals. The principles inherent in any such "interorganiza-

tional network" include *common purposes*, clear lines
of shared *authority*, *incentives* for organizational participation, building and sustaining a *macroculture*, and
interorganizational structure. Homeland security policy
must first ensure that all contributing organizations
share the same overarching common purposes, and
all organizations must accept the respective individual
organizations' divisions of labor within a homeland
security network. Authority, as witnessed in unified
command, must be deferred to the network level, for
both resource allocation and operational command and
control. Incentives, such as goodwill, reciprocation,
budgets, and other resources must flow to member
organizations for their participation. The building
and maintenance of a macroculture must bind people
beyond their "home" organizations. Finally, a clear
interorganizational structure must be formed so that
organizations understand their fit, people understand
their organization's connection to a larger whole, and
channels facilitate the exchange of information up and
down the network chain.

Without an interorganizational network that realizes
joint principles, there will be no sustained and comprehensive national homeland security effort. As the
Gilmore Commission indicated, a homeland security
transition will be difficult, since "a large number of
programs have already been established and may have
to be reconfigured."[24] Pooling organizations that previously operated independently is never easy. Experts
long involved with homeland security issues note that
over the long term even common crises fail to unify
distinct organizations with no shared and overarching
legal mandate to coordinate them.[25] The following
statement in *International Security* accurately describes
the long-term institutional drivers of the status quo:

These actors have distinct interests, budgetary constraints, and legal authority. They are, for the most part, hierarchically organized and have overlapping (or even competing) areas of responsibility.

In many cases, these agencies and organizations have no history of routine interaction, and sometimes have powerful institutional interests working against cooperation or dealing with a new priority imposed by the national security wing of the federal government.[26]

Such sentiment provides both warning and reassurance. Difficult homeland security cultural adjustments most certainly await. But, similar bureaucratic issues applied in the pre-Goldwater-Nichols military. Today's post-Golwater-Nichols system includes cohesive joint policy, doctrine, personnel and staffing, education, training, and unified command. Joint operations now function daily through real interorganizational processes and programs that realize joint principles within a well thought-out design. People have become acculturized and are now beginning to thrive in the new system. Some of the grand goals set forth in the public law are being realized. The jointness ideal is a military, and can also become a homeland security, reality.

Learning from Joint Military Education

One lesson learned throughout Goldwater-Nichols implementation is a most difficult joint principle to realize - the building of a macroculture. And in building that macroculture, the most difficult practical component to achieve is a joint education system. For example, public law, while a challenge in any democratic republic, can be enacted. Agreement in principle can be reached. Policy can reinforce agreement.

Doctrine can support policy. Unified command can be assigned and assumed in accordance with doctrine. Organizations can be mobilized under doctrine through standard operating procedures. All of these things can happen, but the joint experience will fail without deep appreciation, practical know-how, and support of the people who must serve in the joint system. If people are not thoroughly educated in all aspects of what the joint system is set out to do, they will revert back to comfort zones found in their traditional organizations' ways of doing business.

People resist change because they rise through individual organizational structures with shared histories, myths, procedures, and operations to which they attach meaning. Shifting from a focus of employment of resources, assignment of personnel, and establishment of operating procedures from the organizational level to the interorganizational level is traumatic. Such change typically takes a generation. A glance at Goldwater-Nichols implementation reveals senior admirals and generals that grew up in a military service-centric system, which then dramatically shifted to jointness in their mid-careers. The full shift to military jointness may not be thoroughly institutionalized for another decade.

Importantly, education lagged under Goldwater-Nichols and thus necessitated a full generation for joint acculturization. In joint education's beginnings so few military members experienced Phase II joint education[27] because of the time required to build the education pipeline and then put large numbers of students through it. The education lag was exacerbated by a reliance on extensive periods of residential learning that created slots for only a small percentage of military officers. Coupled with the slow education rate was the fact that until the mid-1990's, military officers could bypass joint assignment and still achieve general officer rank. Finally, the initial reluctance of the military services to fully embrace "jointness" in its early years was reflected in internal cultural biases that joint education less favorably compared with service-centric education alternatives.

A generation later there are more (but still too few) officers being thoroughly educated in joint military policy, doctrine, and operations. Even with technology providing opportunities for advanced distributed learning and combinations of adjunct faculty (from the ranks of interagency, subject matter expert, and retired joint military experts) and outsourcing providing an opportunity for the military to expand joint education access, the residential/government-provided education bottleneck still exists. Younger officers continue to be steeped in service-centric education with comparatively little joint education. In short, the joint education system is still evolving.

The Need for a Joint Homeland Security Education System

As in the military experience, education can become the glue that will bind a homeland security macro-culture (see Diagram 1). But, unlike the joint military situation, 16 years of lead-time are not available, and as previously stated, a network of homeland security personnel and organizations span beyond a single profession.

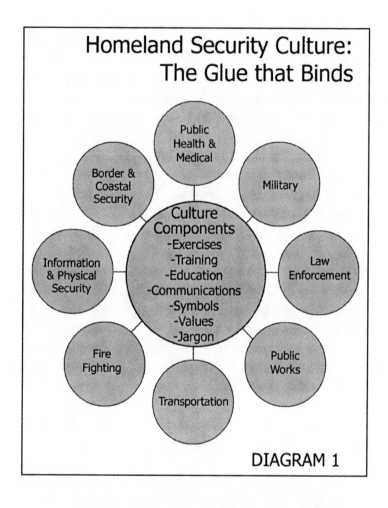

Homeland Security Culture: The Glue that Binds

Public Health & Medical

Border & Coastal Security

Military

Culture Components
-Exercises
-Training
-Education
-Communications
-Symbols
-Values
-Jargon

Information & Physical Security

Law Enforcement

Fire Fighting

Public Works

Transportation

DIAGRAM 1

The first issue of a comprehensive homeland security education system is: *"who would need to be educated?"* The homeland security population includes but is not limited to citizens; first responders; first providers; community representatives; public leaders; federal civil servants; and corporate, non-profit, and voluntary individuals with vested homeland security interests. While these groups will obviously need different types and levels of knowledge, it conservatively totals over 12 million people (and if major groups of loosely affiliated but interested citizens are included, the number is vastly greater). They will first need to learn of those issues that relate directly to their specific homeland security role that may or may not be unique to a function, level, or profession. They will also require a common base of homeland security knowledge that ties them to the network's fundamental principles and operations. At the bottom of specific and common learning will be every participant's understanding of which organization and individual is responsible for what function and how to perform one's own responsibilities on which the rest of a homeland security network will depend.

Participant expectations are critical to a successful education system. For example, the Federal Civil Service Defense Administration (that ran the nation's Cold War civil defense program) assumed the following of its participant, who in this case was the U.S. citizen:

> ...*emotionally unstable, morally irresponsible, and corrupted by leisure, pleasure, and...commodity consumption,'...the public (can) not be trusted to accept the risks of national security deterrence.*[28]

As a result, civil defense education consisted of hierarchical top-down dissemination and offered no opportunity for citizen-students to engage in an educational process. In heavy-handed bureaucratic style, millions of leaflets were mailed without connecting would-be national security participants into a network. Learning occurred in a vacuum with no larger structure into which citizens could affix their thinking.

Contrary to the civil defense experience, a nation

facing a dispersed and mobile (not a single and sta-
tionary) threat cannot maintain the luxury of large
numbers of sideline constituencies. A joint national
system of homeland security must rest on the assumption that citizens, local officials, federal officials,
and other participants will responsibly learn and
implement their roles if properly led to do so. The
system must also heed history's failed national mobilizations, such as the Soviet Union's 1920's experience in
which insufficient leadership, economic, and material
resources led to a functionless paper organization.[29]
Effective joint education systems are focused on
realistic assumptions of what can and cannot be accom-
plished by the people within them.

Some Examples of What Homeland Security Education Could Provide:

Citizen Level

1. AWARENESS: "Communities are demanding to know what's being done to protect them."

2. VIGILENCE: "19 hijackers who carried out the attacks had settled in small communities where they blended in with the locals."

3. CIVIL DEFENSE: "Terrorists were interested in attacking food, power, and water supplies of communities."

4. PLANNING: "An increasing number of cities and towns (are) searching for expertise in putting together crisis management plans..."

5. CONSEQUENCE MANAGEMENT: "It" happened here; now what?[30]

After the "who" and "what" of joint education are identified, the "how" must be implemented. To educate millions is at first glance a seemingly impossible task, and it surely will be if not designed and implemented with foresight. The looming question is: *how will each different form of knowledge be distributed to so many people at so many different levels in so many different functions?* It would be a mistake to focus the delivery of such a complex education and training system on either a traditional government bureaucracy model through the Department of Homeland Security or a government contract model. The bureaucracy model is the knee jerk reaction of every government agency, which in simple terms, would be for the Department of Homeland Security to request funding to expand upon its core homeland security policy and federal function alignment missions to encompass homeland security education and training delivery. The responsibility is simply too cumbersome for a single government department to visualize, manage, and run. And, the answer is not to disperse education and training between the Department of Homeland Security and a myriad other federal departments. This bureaucratic reaction, which is articulated by former CIA director, Robert Gates, should be anticipated:

...while bureaucracies do not have a reputation as hotbeds of creativity, that does not apply to budgeting or protecting turf. The ability of other agencies to craft homeland defense-associated programs that fall outside a specific mandate of the homeland defense office should not be underestimated.[31]

The contractor model focuses on the government's willingness to wash its hands of comprehensive operations or "heavy lifting" and stay only at the concept and requirements level, thereby rewarding and placing responsibility on one or a few contractors to build new joint education expertise at an expensive taxpayer cost. In this model, government would be responsible for identifying only what and who it would like taught at each level and function of government, private industry, academia, non-profits, and citizens at-large. It would most likely pay for the burdensome cost of the initial infrastructure and then the per student costs for each course, seminar, exercise, or learning software taught or used. This model is wasteful and ineffective because it ultimately limits application of many government and non-government capabilities, pays for what already exists, and either places arbitrary limitations on the number of students or cost-prohibitively teaches, trains, or instructs each of them in the system.

Both models only provide portions, and neither captures the essence, of what is required in a shared homeland security education *by design* - a design that must provide an education architecture that will expand and contract based on institutional and student need. For example, foreign terrorism is today's big issue yet domestic terrorism may come back as tomorrow's looming challenge; consequence management is today's response and recovery issue yet natural disaster management may dominate tomorrow's agenda; air travel security is the primary civil security issue today, yet ballistic missile recovery may headline next year's community agenda. All of the issues are important and all must be provided to those that need to know of, prepare for, and participate in them. They share components in common and also possess their own unique attributes. Education must be available in breadth, depth, scope, level, and delivery when, where, and for whom it is needed. No federal-only model will suffice.

A Joint Homeland Security Education Concept

What the nation has at its disposal is a great array of existing homeland security-focused and homeland security-adaptable education and training institutions through which an education system can be realized. These institutions span government, non-government, and corporate forms. It is through the government's collaboration, coordination, and facilitation of such institutions that a powerful "what" can be delivered in a wide variety of means to the "who" wherever one physically and functionally resides in the multi-million student homeland security network. If viewed appropriately as the national resource that such an education network could provide, knowledge building, creation, exchange, research, and dissemination could conceivably begin "tomorrow."

A government example of a homeland security institution that serves as a de facto education "hub" is the U.S. Justice Department's Office of Domestic Preparedness, which provides comprehensive training in awareness, technical, operational, and incident command issues through a consortium of residential instruction providers, to include the Center for Domestic Preparedness (in Anniston, Alabama), New Mexico Institute of Mining and Technology, Louisiana State University, Texas A&M University, and the National Exercise, Test, and Training Center (in Nevada). The Justice Department also runs the Federal Law Enforcement Training Center, which provides residential training to federal and local offices in counterterrorism and other homeland security-related issues. In the past year alone, this Center's capacity has surged from 20,000 to 50,000 students, condensed its curriculum down from 11-week to 9-week course sessions, and increased its training schedule from five to a six days per week.[32]

The Federal Emergency Management Agency (FEMA), through its many educational programs aimed at target-probable areas, already takes responsibility for citizen education surrounding some of the homeland security threat, to include community mitigation and preparation against natural disasters such as wildfires, floods, hurricanes, and earthquakes; protection of life and property during a disaster; and informative ways of accessing federal help after a disaster strikes.[33] FEMA also runs the National Emergency Training Center, which offers a wide range of disaster-focused instruction. The Departments of Defense, Energy, and Health and Human Services and the Environmental Protection Agency also provide extensive homeland security-related education training and education programs. At state and local levels, training and education infrastructure is in place in every major metropolitan and county fire, police, and emergency management system.

Some Examples of What Homeland Security Education Could Provide:

Local Law Enforcement Level

1. Tips for conducing better interviews
2. What to look for in searches
3. How to spot phony credentials
4. What information to pass to the federal level; and when to pass it
5. What questions to ask suspects
6. What to look for to prevent terrorism[34]

Demonstrating its long tradition in national security education and hallmark flexibility in adapting to new challenges, the U.S. Army War College recently introduced full-scale homeland security education and practical exercises for its officer-students. FBI, FEMA, Justice Department, and Pennsylvania Emergency Management Agency representatives assist War College faculty in mock homeland security crises. Also exemplifying the previously identified limitations of joint military education, the 342-student residential war college experience required, in the words of one faculty member, "a big investment in personnel and informational resources to produce the artificial reality."[35]

"It's all about putting the pieces together."[36]

- FBI Special Agent and Counterterrorism Instructor, John Lipke

---

The government programs, both those mentioned above and the many others at federal, state, and local levels, are critical links in homeland security education. These links need to be connected, integrated, and expanded into a comprehensive homeland security education system that meets the dynamic needs of a dramatically increased post-September 11 student pool. While some coordination exists among the federal government education programs, what is lacking is a completely integrated framework through which homeland security-focused curriculum is vetted and approved, students are "cross-town" enrolled, redundancy is avoided completely or is only consciously accepted based on location, capacity, or other justification. The scale of government-provided education also needs to be increased to accommodate many more students from across the homeland security network spectrum. A series of legal or interagency agreements for joint education coordination could coordinate the existing

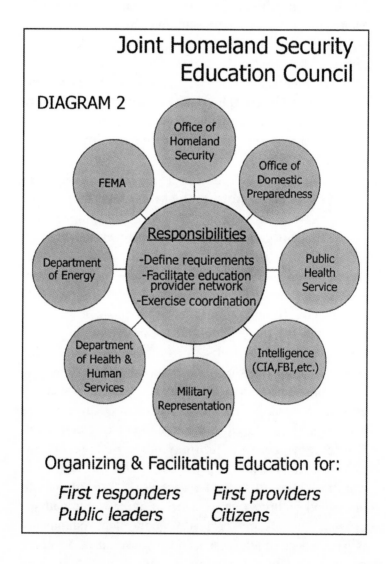

Joint Homeland Security Education Council

DIAGRAM 2

Office of Homeland Security

Office of Domestic Preparedness

FEMA

Responsibilities
-Define requirements
-Facilitate education provider network
-Exercise coordination

Department of Energy

Public Health Service

Department of Health & Human Services

Intelligence (CIA,FBI,etc.)

Military Representation

Organizing & Facilitating Education for:

First responders   *First providers*
Public leaders   *Citizens*

institutions into coherent homeland security education facilitated by the Department of Homeland Security or a National Homeland Security Council at the federal government level. It would also enable all major homeland security government agencies to collectively shape the general curriculum and specifically focus the specialized curricular areas. The mandate could come in the form of a Joint Homeland Security Education Council, which is conceptualized in Diagram 2.

Moving beyond government to further tap the nation's homeland security education potential are a multitude of corporate and private education providers that should be drawn by the proposed Joint Homeland Security Education Council into a joint education network. In a narrow example of how such a system could work, FEMA provides the public with a long list of emergency management and disaster relief education opportunities that are offered by colleges and universities. FEMA also sponsors curriculum and subject matter standards for private institutions to use, such as when the National Fire Academy approved technical, vocational, undergraduate, and graduate fire sciences and management curricula.

If applied for the entire homeland security network, private institutions could identify and comply with homeland security educational requirements through curricular offerings that support the national homeland security education mission. Homeland security personnel could then go through a career experiencing a combination of government-provided, government-facilitated, and government-approved education based on their common and unique education needs at particular points in time. The joint homeland security curriculum would be tracked, analyzed, and maintained for the

student, for his or her home institution at the respective
federal, state, or local level, and for the education-
provider institutions. Practically speaking, students and
institutions would be provided with education portfolios
that could be linked to a homeland security personnel
system - a homeland security human capital system.
In line with President Kennedy's similar but here-
tofore unrealized vision for the 1960's higher federal
civil service,[37] such a network could register, analyze,
identify, and track the nation's homeland security
knowledge in one place, which would facilitate skills
matches against both general and specific homeland security needs during a time of crisis.

Private institutions provide countless examples of
how a coordinated government effort could align with
industry, academia, and non-profit organizations to
further enhance homeland security education, extend
access to millions of students, and track them through
public/private homeland security coordination and
integration. An informal survey of private academic
institutions reveals million-student scaleable residential
and distance education institutions that provide over
2,500 courses and 160 different degree and certificate
programs in national security disciplines to over 50,000
students through over 5,000 faculty members. Included
among the variety of curricula are specific counter
terrorism, consequence management, intelligence, hazardous materials management, information security,
homeland security, and weapons of mass destruction
preparedness programs, to name just a few. The
education is provided for a similar target community
- public health, federal civil service, law enforcement,
fire, emergency medical, emergency management - as
comprises the first responder and provider network.
This existing education architecture can be used as a

medium through which basic knowledge, government training, and academic education can pass. Such information can be fitted into comprehensive programs of professional homeland security education that include relevant academic degrees and certifications in emergency and disaster management, pubic health, homeland security strategy and policy, consequence management, criminal justice, security management, intelligence studies, and terrorism studies, among others. Another type of corporate participation would come through critical thinking, decision making, "click-to-learn," and wargaming technologies that could be integrated into the same education tracking system.

Some Examples of What Homeland Security Education Could Provide: Foreign Language Education across Military, Law Enforcement, Peacekeeping, and Intelligence Organizations
  1. Serbian
  2. Croatian
  3. Creole
  4. Farsi
  5. Pashto[38]

Non-profit and traditional higher education institutions also bring an existing capability through their expert researchers, scientists, policy experts, analysts, and practitioners. These institutions provide homeland security academic journals, newsletters, analytic studies, leader education seminars, homeland security conferences, and exercise simulations. Membership, completion, and participation in such government-sponsored or certified activities can be included in the homeland security human capital databank. This intellectual capability is just one more example among many others from private sources at the government's disposal for joint homeland security education.

"Police Departments are trying to figure out what that (homeland security) means for them. And private industry is moving in to fill the gaps."[39]

- David Carter, Michigan State University Criminologist and Terrorism Expert

---

A convergence of publicly and privately aligned institutions for joint homeland security education in an information sharing; education enhancing; analysis, tracking, reporting, and human capital system would provide the foundation for a macroculture (depicted in Diagram 3) that even the joint military does not yet possess. Such a system has the potential to shave off years if not a generation of know-how in the realization of a joint national homeland security culture. Personnel levels, types, and functions have already been identified. The only thing that remains is the integration of curriculum, professionalization of the force through credentialing and certification, and the participation of joint citizens, first responders, leaders, and other students. Ironically, the Gilmore Commission recommended a *single-source, protected, web-based, integrated information system*.[40] Such a system could be expanded beyond the Commission's intelligence and information tracking intentions to also serve as the homeland security human capital network nucleus by providing a joint information sharing, research, education, and training hub through which students could access education and training.

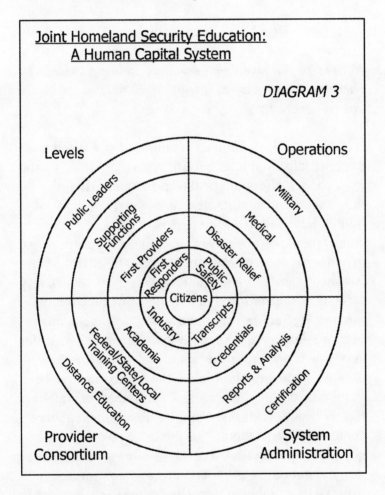

Joint Homeland Security Education:
A Human Capital System

DIAGRAM 3

Levels

Operations

Public Leaders

Supporting Functions

First Providers

Disaster Relief

Military

Medical

First Responders

Public Safety

Citizens

Industry

Transcripts

Academia

Credentials

Federal/State/Local Training Centers

Reports & Analysis

Distance Education

Certification

Provider Consortium

System Administration

A Monumental but Achievable Task

A post-Goldwater-Nichols military has proven that some threats are too vast for any one organization to manage alone, and that pooling disparate capabilities into one system can provide tremendous operational advantages. Thinking similarly, the Office of Homeland Security's Senior Director for Policy and Plans, Richard Falkenrath states:

Although the U.S. domestic preparedness program originated, and is funded, at the federal level, the objectives of the program cannot be achieved solely by pursuing improvements at this level, much less within any one agency.[41]

While the joint military example is not a template over which homeland security may be affixed, the joint model offers applicable principles. If properly introduced and maintained in an interorganizational homeland security network that includes a comprehensive education system at its core, those principles will galvanize American citizens and America's professional response forces to collectively safeguard the nation against the homeland security threat. Reflecting on Thucydides's ancient adage: "There is no need to suppose that human beings differ very much one from the other: but it is true that the ones who come out on top are the ones who have been trained in the hardest school,"[42] and the Federal Law Enforcement Training Center's Paul Hackenberry's contemporary wisdom: "In the end, you are only as good on the street as your mind allows,"[43] it is clear that the nation owes its citizens and communities, as well as its homeland security-focused professionals and organizations, the most cutting-edge knowledge, practical know-how, and effective homeland security education system that all national resources can provide together.

CHAPTER FOUR

A HOMELAND SECURITY RENAISSANCE FOR THE NATIONAL GUARD

The National Guard has been identified as the military's primary component for homeland security from the President down through most every major national security report in recent years - and justifiably so. When considering the needs of national homeland security, the Guard's unique historical, legal, contemporary, and future roles and missions are relatively easy to conjure. What has not been addressed is national security reorganization necessitated by the Guard's potential to become a complete homeland security force. The Guard's transformation into such a force would change the nation's war plans, the other military services, and its own institutional well-being. Most importantly, it would provide homeland security for the American people.

Back to the Future

The National Guard's legacy, a storied tale of state, federal, civil, citizen, and military service, provides historical grist for its contemporary calls to perform military homeland security. It also reflects deep-seated state/federal, local/national, civil/military tensions that an appropriately structured national organization for homeland security could address.[44] The Guard's dueling legacies of varied service and institutional tensions explains its past, present, and future place in the national defense establishment.

A mission-flexible organization whose homeland security nucleus reflects the old volunteer company spirit that led early citizen-leaders such as Ben Franklin to organize community militias, Guard history is filled with dedicated response in many different general-purpose military and civil support roles. 1896, a notable Guard-year in this respect, encapsulates the institution's multifaceted homeland security nature. Guardsmen were summoned on close to 500 different occasions to intervene in lynchings; suppress anti-Chinese riots; enforce newly enacted or controversial state laws; put down civil disorders; control unruly crowds at public events; guard and transport prisoners; resolve religious disputes; aid in fire suppression, response, and recovery; assist in flood operations; enforce public quarantines; and mediate, monitor, and separate industrial warfare disputants.[45]

The Guard's intergovernmental duality was introduced with the Founding Fathers' granting federal authority "for organizing, arming, and disciplining the militia" while reserving officer appointment and militia training responsibilities for the states.[46] Despite a post-Civil War perception of federal primacy through adoption of the Guard's "National" name association, state governors most often employed it. Florida and the federal government together introduced the Guard's modern federal fund/state employ concept in 1887 when the two governments divided drill, armory, summer duty, special duty, and other expenses. This arrangement has evolved to the point where 95% of current Guard funding comes from the federal government.[47]

Frequent citizen-militia styled parade, drill, field exercise, and crisis response forged a close relationship between the public and the Guard, the latter becoming an extension of the former.[48]   In a tradition that continues to present day, Guard leaders, organizations, and facilities served as centers of community social and political life.[49]   Itself an extension of the community, Congress naturally embraced the Guard and has remained a strong proponent.   Not afraid to keep national security politics local, former congressman Mickey Edwards commented of legislative favor bestowed on the Guard: "It's people in your community.   I would be much more responsive to that than to what the Pentagon was requesting."[50]   Nineteenth-century Guardsman, Major General Alfred Pearson summarized the Guard-community essence, when he said:

Meeting an enemy on the field of battle, you go there to kill...But here you (have) men with fathers and brothers and relations mingled in the crowd...[51]

Service in the community, even in uncomfortable roles, was accepted by the citizenry and its representatives because the Guard - *their* Guard - was the community itself.

If state employment of local citizens in community support is a first theme running through history, federal ambiguity is a second.   That ambiguity is tied, not to the Guard's homeland security mission that the executive branch has steadfastly supported, but to its involvement in military operations overseas.   Executive branch uncertainty first manifested in War Department worries over Guard legal authority, readiness, and professionalism to fight in the Spanish-American War.

Secretary of War Elihu Root proposed for the Guard
a place, but not a full place, in national defense.[52]
General McClellan reflected a federal bias that professionals fight wars and citizen-soldiers protect homes,
when he planned for Guardsmen "to protect the coasts
of the U.S." in the face of a looming three-front war.[53]
Although the Guard eventually served admirably
overseas in Spanish-American, both World, and Korean
Wars, some form of McClellan's homefront bias held
and was reinforced through a Cold War emphasis on the
professional soldier. This thinking culminated during
Vietnam, when Guard leadership sought their units'
deployment overseas but instead saw them called out
72 times for domestic riot control over a two-decade
period.[54] The Vietnam argument described by historian
John Mahon summarizes the historical warfighting ambiguity and homeland security support:

*It was impossible to make an efficient national
instrument out of fifty-two state oriented military estab-
lishments which already had the mission of helping to
preserve internal order and mitigating human suffering
caused by flood, fire, drought, snow, and wind.*[55]

Tug-of-War

Adopted in the 1970's amid intense internal debate,
the Department of Defense's Total Force Policy
removed - on paper - federal doubts of Guard combat
participation. An assumption that peacetime professionals could not support modern war demands,[56] and
a tightened federal budget, led to the policy still reflected today.[57] Retaining its comfort with the Guard's
homeland role, the Department of Defense added significant national military strategy responsibilities.

Today, the Guard is clearly a federal defense asset first and stateside civil support organization second.[58] Warfighting primacy is reflected in the Guard's own rank order of its societal roles:

The National Guard has two roles - one as part of the nation's entire military force, and the other to the respective states for emergency response and community support missions.[59]

While the Total Force Policy has capably underpinned three decades of national military strategy, its inherent federal dominance of the Guard has created a two-fold problem. First, in making the warfight predominant, the Guard is resourced for roles it must vigilantly prepare for yet not often implement, while the constancy of its annual missions are homeland responses. Second, the sheer volume of state and federal expectations and subsequently attractive federal monies associated with them assures that the Guard will valiantly try to do all missions well, yet will inevitably fall short on some.

Concerning the predominant societal role, it is clear that federal warfighting requirements do not neatly align with stateside missions. The 1997-2001 diagrams of the nation's largest Guard contingent - the California Army National Guard - reveals the fundamental differences. Generally, state and federal homeland security missions tend to be unpredictable - down to mere days or even hours to respond - and involve small, rapidly mobilized group or team deployments. Federal warfighting missions are less frequent, provide longer lead times, require extensive unit training, and involve significantly larger unit deployments for much lengthier periods of time. Mission disparities are reflected in the

California Guard's internal reporting and analysis, with state missions tracked in man-days deployed and federal missions tracked in unit-days deployed.

The disparity in warfighting and homeland security mission-types raise important issues for both readiness and organizational design. First, it is logical to assume that any military organization faced with immediate challenges, such as responding to real crises when ordered to do so by state or federal authorities, will deal with those crises prior to preparing for future missions, such as those outlined in the national military strategy. So, while warfighting primacy may exist on paper, stateside support is the Guard's predominant reality.

Second, the federal power projection role has forced the Guard to organize in large dispersed units with associated warfighting assets versus smaller, geographically coordinated units with tailored assets and personnel skill-sets more appropriately aligned with homeland security needs. One example is the 29th Separate Infantry Brigade, which maintains its headquarters and an infantry battalion in Hawaii, an infantry battalion in California, a Reserve infantry battalion in Hawaii (with one company in Guam and two companies in American Samoa), a cavalry troop in Oregon, and an air defense battery in Minnesota. While scripted together in national war plans, these units' homeland security employment could require operational and administrative coordination among five civil authorities and two federal authorities. A notable exception to such cumbersome design is the Guard's 22-member homeland security-scripted Weapons of Mass Destruction Civil Support Teams. Not surprisingly, these teams have been recommended to double in size by a recently published report sponsored by the Council on Foreign Relations.[60]

California Army National Guard Warfighting/MOOTW:
Year/Mission/Unit-Days of the Response

Mission Type	1997	1998	1999	2000	2001
Law	10	17	6,159	1,391	76
Fire	-	246	10,456	4,897	2,949
Search/Rescue	32	146	167	89	122
Flood	14,180	14,452	33	-	3
Civil Support	-	674	122	77	42
Noble Eagle*	-	-	-	-	764*
Other	-	-	-	-	-
Total Days (# of missions)	14,222 (8)	15,535 (19)	16,973 (43)	6,454 (23)	3,192 (39)

Note: Information provided by Plans, Operations, and Security section of the California National Guard. Author interpretation of time spent in specific missions may inadvertently lead to minor discrepancies.

*Federal homeland security operation tracked in unit-days of response and not included in "total days" or "#" of missions summaries.

California Army National Guard Warfighting/MOOTW:
Year/Mission/Unit-Days of the Response

Mission Type	1997	1998	1999	2000	2001
Germany	125	-	-	-	-
Bosnia	19	115	48	30	-
Kosovo	125	-	-	11	-
Southwest Asia	-	-	-	-	134
Total Days (# of missions)	144 (2)	115 (1)	48 (1)	41 (2)	898 (1)

Note: Information provided by Mobilization and Readiness section of the California National Guard. Author interpretation of time spent in specific missions may inadvertently lead to minor discrepancies.

The second Total Force issue is the institutional strain created by two primary roles. No other military organization is so burdened at home and abroad. There is obviously a limit to the number of state and federal missions that overwhelmingly part-time personnel averaging 39 training days per year[61] can train for and respond to at any given time without sacrificing mission effectiveness. It is also clear from the diagrams above that state missions swing widely from year-to-year and thus guarantee no fixed amount of training time enjoyed by other military forces.

Total Force is perpetuated because of the many federal resources available for state and local redeployment. The higher a federal priority in wartime missions, the more resources a particular Guard unit receives.[62] Federal, state, and Guard authorities know that resources are tied to one mission yet used for another. Guard and state leaders inevitably feel pressure to protect their own assets vis-à-vis other states instead of working to appropriately align their state and the total Guard as a comprehensive local, state, regional, and national security asset. This issue was highlighted recently in *USA Today*:

> *They (Guard leaders) fear that the federal government will shift their understaffed units, and potentially millions of dollars, to states that can recruit enough troops to fill them.*[63]

Total Force pulls the Guard in many directions at home and abroad before it even responds to its first stateside crisis or sends its first soldier in harm's way, and it translates into long term readiness, recruitment/ retention, and leadership trends. Regarding readiness, the Guard is not prepared to effectively fulfill its federal warfighting missions. Taking its top unit, the Enhanced Brigade, the General Accounting Office (GAO) reported in 1995 that units were well short of training, recruitment, and retention levels.[64] While improving slightly, a 2000 GAO follow-on report concluded 3 of 15 brigades failed mission-essential maneuver tasks, 14 of 15 brigades failed to meet staffing goals, and 10 of the brigades' 24 mechanized battalions failed gunnery standards.[65] Mirroring the experience of the brigades are the previously mentioned weapons of mass destruction civil support teams, which, after three years and $143 million still have serious equipment and installation failures.

Readiness shortfalls were attributed by Guard commanders as having far too much to do across the non-sequitorial spectrum of federal and state missions. The GAO concluded of the brigades: "their potential missions are many and varied and expanding"[66] and "to ask all the brigades to be ready for all missions all the time creates a climate of unrealistic expectations."[67]

Institutional tensions reflect in people. The strain of so many missions adversely affects retention and recruitment, as described by the National Guard Association: "As...members experience more frequent and lengthy mobilizations and deployments, recruiting and retaining skilled personnel...become proportionally more difficult."[68]

Guard leaders reflect the tension as well. Adjutants-general, while preparing for war plans in support of federal authority and in receipt of federal resources, respond to state crisis management needs and are appointees of state governors (except in two cases where they are directly elected).[69] Placed between both ends of the political system, strong Guard leaders use the common state-federal platform to serve both causes, while others opportunistically manipulate it for their own purposes. Guard adjutants-general commit sexual misconduct, coercion, harassment, financial impropriety, perjury, and misuse of government property at twice the rate of regular Army and Air Force generals.[70]

Mission-resource tension has also led Guard leaders to report misleading attendance for non-drilling Guard members. Describing the potential outcome of such misrepresentation, a retired Illinois Guardsman's view also summarizes the systematic unreality created by Total Force federal expectations and stateside homeland responses:

The real harm is when units get called up, and...we have given a grossly false picture...when we get to combat, and we are not ready, the unit pays the price, and the nation pays the price.[71]

The current design provides no mechanism for formal corrective action. Former Clinton administration budget Director Leon Panetta observes, "absent any national scandal...there's almost an intimidation not to do the kind of oversight that needs to be done."[72]

The Renaissance

Its dual-role nature as a citizen-soldier and state-federal hybrid institution positions the Guard at the nexus between the profession of arms - which is by its nature removed by a set of standards and a calling apart from the society in which it serves - and traditional civil defense - which is composed of civilians-in-arms. To straddle the nexus between professional and citizen is to compromise some of each in order to gain the benefits of both. What this means is that the Guard never will reach, and should never be expected to reach, the level of military readiness and battlefield proficiency of the active force. But, it also means that the active force will never attain the unique relationship and response capability that the Guard enjoys among America's communities. The best fit for the Guard in the national security establishment is where the local/national, military/civilian, professional/political spheres intersect, which is precisely where homeland security falls.

On the flip side of the equation is the active component, a group of purely professional military organizations distinct from the rest of society. Viewing homeland security as a distraction from power projection and warfighting,[73] Secretary of the Army Thomas White articulates the issue as a problem of concurrency: "The Army is fully deployed...we don't need to volunteer for any other tasks."[74] This view was seconded in the *National Journal*:

> *...elected politicians historically had to push the Pentagon into taking on domestic roles, whether in the war on drugs, border control, or training local firefighters and police for antiterrorism efforts. Driven both by a high-minded devotion to civilian control over the military and by a pragmatic reluctance to take on messy domestic missions, the military in general scrupulously adheres to the spirit of the 1878 Posse Comitatus Act, which forbids the U.S. military from enforcing U.S. laws.*[75]

The winning political, legal, and organizational solution for the active component, Guard, and general national security interests is to divide national military labor. The Guard should focus on those capabilities that fall most securely on the faultline between military professional and citizen servant. The active and reserve forces should focus on capabilities that fall clearly within the sphere of military professional. The division translates to a focus of the Guard exclusively on roles and missions "over here" and a focus of the active and reserve forces on missions "over there."

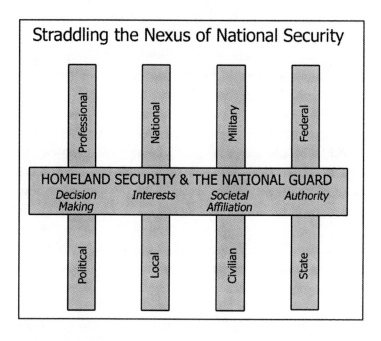

The evolution of national security abroad harkens back to former Secretary of Defense Robert McNamara's belief that his times called for quick response units and not "untrained Guardsmen" for expeditionary operations overseas.[76] The entire military is transforming into a technologically advanced and expeditionary operation - Army Transformation to light and rapidly deployable forces, Air Expeditionary Forces, and the Marine Corps expeditionary force-in-readiness. In a transformed military, the existing gap between expedient and follow-on forces will only grow as doctrine, training, and technology combine to reduce space/time issues of military engagement. In this power projection evolution, there is no longer a place for a part- and lengthy lead-time component. The Army Reserve, ideally situated for follow-on power projection requirements under completely federal authority, could assume current Guard combat requirements through extensive use of the effective multi-component (i.e.: active and reserve) command concept down to the battalion level.

A homeland security-focused Guard would align with the evolving security environment and the rest of the national security establishment. September 11 was not an isolated incident. Indicating as much before that fateful day, the U.S. Commission on National Security for the 21st Century concluded that the essence of war will not change - there will be casualties, carnage, and death - but, significantly, the actors will change.[77] In that environment, the different actors and their new technologies require "different military and other national capabilities."[78]

Part of a national capability will be expeditionary military operations at home, which translates into a traditional force-in-readiness Guard with a 21st Century design. But, building national capability is greater than the Guard, so it is important to identify potential roles for the lead military homeland security force. Guard roles should follow historical precedent in supporting - not leading - local, regional, and federal civil authorities. Ideal roles should also be limited to those requiring domestic military response. The standard for Guard use should be (a) when military force or response is necessary or (b) when no other organization can respond in as timely a manner until other resources can be mobilized. Other homeland security missions should fall to organizations in federal or state response plans that are functionally aligned with the threat - public health, law enforcement, wildland fire, emergency management, among others. Use of the Guard would follow once initial response capacities have been reached or in purely support missions.

The following section proposes major roles and missions that a homeland security-focused Guard could provide.

General Purpose Homeland Security Force

Threats to the homeland are still emerging and will continue to surprise. The challenge, as articulated by Secretary of Defense Donald Rumsfeld, "is a difficult one: to defend our nation against the unknown, the uncertain, the unseen, the unexpected."[79] Surprise is countered with general purpose force possessed with flexible response capability. The Guard's primary mission will be to "be ready" as a homeland security force-in-readiness. Recommended by the U.S. Commission on National Security for the 21st Century, the Guard should possess a rapid reaction capability that could be quickly mobilized with command and control capabilities for multiple forms of emergency.[80] As a homeland security force-in-readiness, the Guard must be expected to take the job no one thought of, provide the response created out of the next crisis that was never planned, and perform the thankless duty available only in a force-in-readiness. Eventually, such roles that do not require a standing military requirement should be transferred, but the Guard may be the only option in the heat of the moment. Building and maintaining such a capability would require a higher percentage of full-time Guard forces, since the Guard would be expected to be among the "first on scene."

Consequence Management

There are several societal weapons of mass destruction consequences of which at least four depend on timeliness and justify immediate military response: massive casualties, contamination, panic, and degraded response capabilities.[81] They also align with necessary Guard-like operational capability: incident command and communications, emergency medical treatment, decontamination of individuals and facilities, security and crowd control, apprehension of perpetrators, special weapons and tactics operations, special weapons disablement, hazardous materials management, infectious disease surveillance and control, plume analysis, medical care for victims, public affairs, mass transportation and large-scale emergency logistics, and legal affairs.[82] Within the operational capability are critical Guard-associated tasks: imposition and enforcement of a curfew; temporary detention or location restriction of the public; military law enforcement, population control, and logistics; seizure of property for hospital, utilities, medical, vehicular, transit, and other purposes; forced public decontamination or vaccination; censure of the media; citizen search and seizure; disposal of the deceased; and forced civilian labor.[83] Adding to the tasks, the Commission on National Security recommended "participate and initiate, where necessary, state, local, and regional planning for responding to a weapons of mass destruction incident; train and help organize local first responders; maintain up-to-date inventories of military resources and equipment available

in the area on short notice; (and) plan for rapid interstate support and reinforcement..."[84]

Emergency Management

Even prior to September 11, the Guard's emergency
response capability was the first priority among state
and local civil leaders. Representative of several recommendations to more closely link the Guard to the
Federal Emergency Management Agency's (FEMA's)
role in emergency management, a 1999 bill led by
Senator Ted Stevens (R-AL) directed what have become
joint FEMA-Guard training exercises.[85] In emergency
management the states should retain their constitutionally provisioned authority, with FEMA as the
primary federal component to provide supplementary
assistance in overwhelming situations. The Guard, politically dual-purposed by design, co-located where any
homeland emergency will unfold, and expeditionary,
should plan on, train for, and respond in support of both
state and federal emergency management authorities.
The Guard should naturally supplant the current
Reserve's FEMA-military emergency management
liaison responsibility.

Counterdrug Operations

Although a disputed and on-again, off-again use of
the Guard, counterdrug operations are authorized under
Title 32 so long as they do not "degrade the (military)
training and readiness of such units and personnel."[86]
As long as counterdrug policy, strategy, and operations
are a national priority, they should be considered a
homeland security issue and the Guard a counterdrug
support asset for coordinated use with law enforcement

agencies. Guard counterdrug involvement should be focused almost exclusively on those roles that expand beyond law enforcement capabilities.

Public Health Support

The state of public health systems at state and local levels is deplorable. They lack qualified medical personnel, medical resources, and physical assets and infrastructure. The Guard is uniquely postured to fill this void by providing physical and logistical support required in single and multi-state public health operations, and it is also capable of aligning in interstate agreements among its own member organizations and with non-military organizations. Public health tasks for the Guard should include support of civil authorities in early detection and on-site treatment, separation or quarantine, control of roads and public areas, security of facilities, and physical site access, among others.[87] The acts should provide mutual aid through interstate compacts as a critical regional emergency provision.[88]

Public Law Enforcement

The Guard's historic public law enforcement missions should continue, and they should be improved to meet new challenges. Such missions include but are not limited to enforcement of quarantines, crowd control, civil rights enforcement, riot suppression, and industrial security. Using the Guard to enforce public laws provides an opportunity for compliance with the Posse Comitatus Act of 1878 if the Guard were linked through state mutual aid agreements.

Territorial Integrity

Border defense is a federal mission against which the Guard should continue to be Title 10-deployed, and it is a state issue that should continue to be Title 32-authorized. Other agencies should take the lead in border defense with the Guard available for extraordinary operations and circumstances.

Homeland Security Civil Support Roles & Missions

Public Health

Consequence Management

Public Order

Border Security

National Guard Roles

Enforcing Public Law

Industrial Security

Continental Airspace Security

Other Duties As Directed

National Guard Missions:

- Counterdrug operations
- Riot suppression
- National missile defense
- National air defense
- Industrial security
- Emergency management
- Wildland firefighting support

- Border patrol
- Coastal defense
- Quarantine
- WMD response
- WMD training
- General purposes
- Crowd control

Coastal defense is an historic Guard mission outlined in Title 32,[89] and it should be coordinated among other organizations involved in coastal and maritime defense and access, such as the Navy, Coast Guard, and Customs Service.

Aerospace and national missile defense are logical missions for the Guard to either outrightly assume or participate in as the lead military homeland security force.

Context of the Renaissance

The homeland security organization into which the Guard should administratively fit includes the integration of emergency management, territorial integrity, transportation security, public health, information security, and other functions. This organization should go a step beyond President Bush's initial homeland security blueprint and place the Guard under the Department of Homeland Security. Although a civil-military force, the Guard should be housed among its federal homeland security neighbor institutions that it will most frequently support. The Guard would continue to draw on Army and Air Force training, equipment, and assets through interdepartmental agreements.

Under such an arrangement, the Guard would need a four-star flag officer as its chief. Creation of a four-star Guard leader is not new and was proposed during the 1996-1997 Quadrennial Defense Review.[90] Redesigning the Guard's federal authority under a four-star officer with authority over recruitment, training, organization, and equipment for federal missions would provide federal organization of national military homeland security missions.

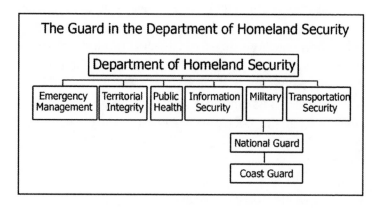

The Guard's administrative integration should co-incide with its operational employment at the core of the U.S. Northern Command, the authority of which spans all domestic federal military operations.[91] The arrangement of the politically adept Guard as the Northern Command's core military component will assist the Northern Command's Commander-in-Chief (CINC) with what journalist Stanley Freedberg high-lights as a pressing challenge:

Any CINC for the new Northern Command...(has) to deal every day with...governors, senators, and rep-resentatives from all 50 states...as ticklish as any other regional commander's job may be, a northern com-mander (has) to operate at an even higher octave of political sensibility.[92]

The new CINC will face the Guard's centuries-old political tug-of-war. Having the Guard on board will assist in political consensus-building at federal, re-gional, state, and local levels.

Beyond the federal organization the Guard's state-federal response capabilities are essential. Biological incidents, for example, have the potential to span from one state to others, which could transition a response from state to federal level in the middle of a crisis due to interstate commerce implications.[93] Whether under state or federal authority the Guard can legally respond, and such an intergovernmental capability should be leveraged under the Northern Command through specific tasking and resourcing for general and specialized Guard unit missions. All types of missions - federal, regional, state, local - should be harnessed for state and national application through a tight arrangement of public law, interstate memoranda, and mutual aid compacts. As stated by the Office of Homeland Security's Dr. Richard Falkenrath, "this should involve some explicit compact, perhaps embodied in legislation, between the federal and state and local governments on their respective responsibilities for building and maintaining preparedness."[94] Leading the need to work together, President Bush says:

We've got to strengthen security in small-town America...by helping smaller communities and smaller counties develop what we call 'mutual aid agreements'...One town may have a good hospital, another may be able to lend fire trucks, a third may have hazardous material experts...We've got to develop these mutual pacts so that we can coordinate efforts (and) pool resources.[95]

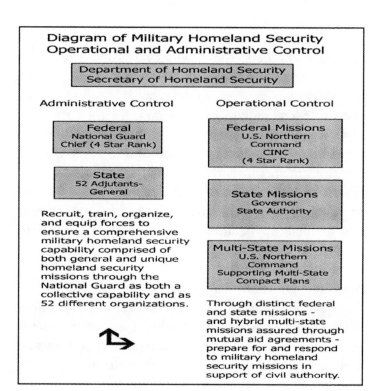

Ties to National Service

In his efforts to strengthen America, President Bush has called Americans to "stand strongly in the face of evil,"[96] and he has pledged citizens' participation in the defense of their homeland through creation of the citizen-centered $230 million USA Freedom Corps and $144 million Citizen Corps councils.[97] Although 25,000 people have signed on to the Citizen Corps mission to identify homeland security threats and resources, develop community action plans, and communicate and collaborate with other voluntary organizations and state and federal agencies, there is also great potential for Citizen Corps and Guard cooperation. Citizen Corps will include "leaders from law enforcement,

fire and emergency medical services, businesses, com-
munity-based institutions, schools, places of worship,
health care facilities, public works, and other key community sectors."[98] Their missions include performing
non-sworn police functions to get more cops on the
street, augmenting health care capacity in emergencies,
feeding information into a street-level terrorist information reporting system, responding as emergency
responders, performing neighborhood watch, and preparing for catastrophe in accordance with standardized
citizen preparedness guidebooks.[99]

Mission-linked with homeland security and re-in-
vigorated with a new found sense of national security
purpose, the Guard could also be tethered as a cornerstone USA Freedom Corps initiative, both as an
organization that volunteering citizens could assist
through backline support operations and as an institution to serve for two or three years of national, state,
and community service. Currently, USA Freedom
Corps promotes the military in general as a vehicle
towards citizen-service, but its coordinated cornerstone
institutions do not include the military and are limited to
international development (i.e.: Peace Corps), education
and public well-being initiatives (i.e.: Americorps;
Learn and Serve America), intergenerational community
service (i.e.: Senior Corps), and domestic security
support (i.e.: Citizen Corps). For volunteering citizens
in support roles, ideas to use citizens in the Guard's
armory maintenance and family readiness counseling
programs should be implemented and broadened to
many other areas.

Linking service in the community-oriented Guard
alongside teaching, inner city volunteerism, public
safety, and other noble service initiatives ties with the
views of esteemed military sociologist, Dr. Charles

Moskos. He states, "this is the first time in our history we're entering a war of significant size and probably duration without drafting young men to fight the threat."[100] Believing "the terrorist threat will force us to confront our notion of citizenship," Moskos calls for a sustained citizen homefront commitment across all public service sectors. A homeland security National Guard would be an ideal institution through which to realize twenty-first century citizen service.

The Guard in an American Citizen-Service Fabric

A transformation of the Guard to homeland security will solidify its twenty-first century place in the traditional American fabric. For the first time in over a generation, the Guard would be positioned, not only as a primary institution for national security, but also as a popularly accepted national service opportunity for large numbers of high school graduates before or during college or while otherwise employed in the civilian economy. Unlike the current view of a Guardsman's life, which according to former Reserve Affairs director, Steven Duncan, is "...only a quick telephone call away from active duty in a potentially hostile environment,"[101] one's entire life would not be completely uprooted to perform homeland security service. Enlistees would stay close to home while honorably serving their community and learning leadership and highly technical skills. Working among fire, police, emergency medical, military, information security, intelligence, public health, and emergency management professions would provide deep appreciation of citizen-service and practical post-service employment opportunities.

Divide and Conquer

In his national homeland security strategy, President Bush thrice supports reorganization.[102] The reorganization should be implemented with care previous reorganizations were given, to include the Total Force Policy, which articulated a timeless goal: "to determine the most advantageous mix to support national strategy and meet the threat."[103] What President Bush and the Total Force Policy recognize(d) in respectively different times is the fact that when the fundamental threat to society changes, society must reorganize to meet the threat.

While perhaps easy to propose and logical to consider, the actual task of reorganization is huge. But, the status quo speaks as well, particularly for the Guard. As indicated in multiple General Accounting Office reports to Congress, homeland security spans civil and military national security missions, and there are many organizations at federal, state, and local levels already preparing to respond redundantly in place of potential

Guard missions.[104] If the Guard is not boldly moved
to assume the predominant portion of the military's
homeland security role, other civilian and military organizations will fill the void, and the Guard's institutional
fault lines will force it to incongruously flop between
warfighting and civil support. It will do neither with
great expectation, and over the long term it will fail
to the point of utter redundancy and irrelevancy. At
such a point, even the congressional vote for "people
in your community"[105] will be turned on its head as the
American people and its communities are better served
by institutional arrangements both overseas and at
home that will provide embarrassingly superior service
in their core competencies as compared to a torn organization trying to serve part-time duty to two full-time
responsibilities.

Dividing military homeland and power projection
labor between the National Guard and the active and
reserve forces will alleviate institutional tensions
by aligning military organizations around core
competencies and positioning them in their appropriate
places in the national security structure. The Guard's
niche would take a generation to fully evolve, but
eventually it would reach a status of equality among
national security partner organizations. Its unspoken
but very real perception as a "lesser among equals" in
the national military establishment would be forever
shed. Permanently marking the Guard for homeland
security would halt the dilution of Army, Navy, Air
Force, and Marine Corps roles and missions away from
expeditionary power projection overseas. In the end the
reorganization would be marked as the beginning of a
true renaissance - and not just for the Guard - for the
nation.

CHAPTER FIVE

THE UNITED STATES POSTAL SERVICE AND HOMELAND SECURITY

"Can you name one person who visits your house every day of the week – except Sundays and holidays?"[106]

- *Mail Call*, a children's book about the U.S. Postal Service by Nancy O'Keefe Bolick

When astrophysicist and author David Brin envisioned a fictitious post-holocaust American future, he rallied a struggling nation around an institutional image to begin a process of reawakening. Leading the nation out of a dark age of clan rivalry and brute survival, *The Postman* answers heroism's call only reluctantly - but answer the call he does. In America's response to terrorism and efforts to regain a long-term sense of security at home, the U.S. Postal Service should be reconsidered as an organization of public servants who perform national service. Building on the Post's ubiquitous local presence, prestigious national security heritage, federal system, and national structure, President Bush has identified it as a support element in his homeland security strategy. This paper addresses how that strategy's implementation could unlock the post's homeland security support potential.

Homeland Security Strategy and the Post

Encompassing a series of initiatives in an evolving homeland security strategy that direct or strongly encourage frontline homeland security roles for government, non-government, and voluntary organizations, President Bush's USA Freedom Corps aligns and strengthens previously independent organizations such as Americorps and the Peace Corps, proposes new programs, and pulls together seemingly disparate citizen groups such as young teachers and elderly volunteers under a common national service rubric. USA Freedom Corps also includes a proposed but now embattled Terrorist Information and Prevention System (TIPS) and an expansion of neighborhood watch programs with an anti-terrorism focus. The Freedom Corps cornerstone initiative - Citizen Corps Councils - incorporates local law enforcement, fire and emergency medical service, business, school, and church leaders as homeland security organizers.

In his strategy the President plans for postal "involve(ment) as appropriate," working with their "state and local counterparts to help support the work of the (Citizen Corps) Councils."[107] He also loosely ties the Postal Service into the TIPS plan, envisioning its thousands of letter carriers as part of an information reporting system along with transport workers, truckers, train conductors, ship captains, and utility employees. Organizing these uniquely positioned people to recognize and report suspicious activity, the federal government would provide every participant with a toll-free phone number on a vehicle reporting sticker.[108] Aside from consideration as an appropriate Citizen Corps resource and TIPS participant, there are no other homeland security plans for the Postal Service.

Notably, it is not included in the expanded anti-terrorism neighborhood watch program.

A Bigger Role

The post is a pervasive American institution, and as such, its role in this new kind of war must be more substantially considered. That it is at all incorporated in homeland security planning is a testament to the Bush Administration's comprehensive approach. With the proliferation of information technologies, the post is overlooked in contemporary society. Even prior to the Internet in 1972, a postal historian recognized a growing "national myopia" towards the post, "betrayed by the fact that...abundant...'communications'...with radio and television, allow us to forget the central role of the mail in the history of American life."[109] Acknowledging the myopia, former Postmaster General James Farley observed, "far too many Americans take (the Postal Service) for granted. They shrug it off as a necessary but boring presence in our day-to-day existence."[110]

Although reduced to society's mundane backdrop, the letter carrier remains a most ubiquitous public presence, the post still firmly entrenched as a national asset. At the same time Farley spoke of the post's being taken for granted, he observed it as:

> ...the most human of our national institutions. Every person...needs its daily service...(it) touches more people, in a more personal way, and more often, than does any other agency of our government. It is essential to our way of life.[111]

Speaking in 1870 of its universal appeal, Senator Charles Sumner timelessly observed, "of all departments, the post office is...the most universal in its beneficence...there is nothing which is not helped by the post office."[112]

No other societal institution so broadly extends across the whole of America. The post is the only intercultural and intergovernmental institution integrated into every major aspect of American life - economic, social, religious, political, law enforcement, health, social services, and military.[113] Unlike fire, police, military, utility, cable, Internet, political, or any other public service, the Postal Service visits every home, community, and organization every day of the year (including Sundays and holidays with Express Mail service). While Americans may send 50 emails for every letter or bill they mail, their letter carrier still exchanges with them over 680 million pieces of daily mail.[114] Those exchanges also still provide a primary government-citizen conduit to disseminate information through the post's traditional role as a "clearing house for American democracy."[115]

Early Postal History and State Security

In light of the national myopia towards the post, any substantial homeland security role for it must first be considered against the backdrop of historical postal contributions to national security. While occasionally at odds with United States constitutionally endowed freedoms, postal history is a near exclusive study of state survival. It reveals the post as a military, communications, economic, law enforcement, and frontier security support institution.

Originating early in recorded history, not to provide today's citizen-to-citizen communications, but to promote and defend state interests, the post emerged among public functions as an irreplaceable national security institution. Witnessed in the postal-deficient Dark Ages, the building and maintenance of a strong post and the survival of a state went hand-in-hand. Ancient Persia established the concept of building and maintaining a strong postal system in 500 B.C., when it extended a royal road stocked with fleet-footed horses at fourteen-mile intervals. This system delivered governmental command and control edicts. Egypt, in adding to its routes a cadre of police guards for postal security, established a postal dual-use precedent by adopting its secure posts as state safe havens. The Egyptian post also effectively linked reining nobility with military outposts and thus ensured two-way intelligence reporting and information flow between the capital and empire.[116] Japanese and Chinese posts served similar government and military purposes, but they included separate private courier systems for commercial and private mail.[117] The Romans used a widely dispersed post as a commercial logistics and military foundation to expand the empire. This highly advanced system piggybacked on an extensive military roads network and contributed to commercial mobility, transfer of strategic military reserves, dissemination of central government information, reporting of intelligence, and communications with, between, and among farflung frontier provinces.[118]

Costly to build and maintain, and indirect in the societal return on investment, only the state could afford such extensive postal operations. And, only the state could assure the authority of postal communications. Letters were sealed to protect state information. Privacy was sacrificed to the state in times of peril. Noted by historian Carl Steele, the "sanctity of the mails" was respected in times of peace but ceded in times of state unrest.[119] To secure the mail was to guard against anti-state interests.

The act of delivering mail from sender to recipient was also a traditional security issue. Establishing a long-held historical precedent, early postal resources were transferred during unrest from commercial and citizen service to those of national defense. This need, to not only deliver mail, but to also ensure its safety and message security on behalf of the state, predated the United States and led early colonial leaders such as Ben Franklin to create a secure mail system that could unite disparate colonies towards independence.[120] That system later evolved into the first federal government organization - the Post Office Department of the United States.[121]

The Post and U.S. National Security

Of the post's contributions through 250 years of American history, 1990's Postmaster General Marvin Runyon reflected:

We were America's 'first information superhighway,' linking distant communities by letter across trails and dusty roads. Over the decades the Postal Service has helped make our nation a...world power. We are the strong and enduring thread that holds the fabric of our nation together.[122]

Ruynon's observation of the post as a "strong and enduring thread" reflects its contributions to national interests as a disseminator of information, facilitator of economic growth, and leader towards continental settlement and infrastructure development.

Scattered around the eastern seaboard during the American Revolution, politicians and military leaders depended on the mail more than any other public function to coordinate policy and strategy. Providing a vital and reliable mode of speedy communications between Congress and the armies, postmasters and mail riders were exempted from military duty.[123] Special couriers were hired to carry Congressional messages; service boats were employed for coastal delivery.[124] Whether afloat or afoot, they dodged bullets and suffered an enemy army's harsh judgment when captured.

Continuing as an arm of national defense up to and through the Civil War, postal decisions followed military needs at both strategic and tactical levels. Even prior to the war, postal route selection was based on the North's need to secure and maintain communications advantage over the South.[125] After hostilities commenced, small town Union post offices and military postmasters general facilitated news from the front to the home and vice versa and thus kept morale high on the front lines and information flowing back to the homefront network.[126]

Continental expansion and protection, the nineteenth century's other overarching national security concern, also provided the post a leading role, in this case as information facilitator, economic agent, and regional uniter. President James Buchanan called for a nation united "by a chain of Americans which can never be broken"[127] at a time when citizens on the frontier lacked communications back east for word of family, community, national developments, or government direction. The post provided indications and warnings against potential western succession and foreign nations' hostile claims to western lands.[128]

At times both leading and following overland development from the eastern seaboard to California, the post provided the only means of linking a scattered America as Buchanan's "unbreakable chain." Over a century of development, private and public postal operations dotted the whole of the continent and reached 18,000 offices and hundreds more on mobile rail, steam, and stage operations.[129] Contracted mail operations, such as those run by Wells Fargo, provided offices in every town, messengers on every steamboat, and officials on every rail and stage operation. Postmaster General Ebenezer Hazard flooded western citizens with newspapers, letters, and government announcements to keep the nation informed at all of its disparate points.

The post also facilitated economic development, expansion, and security through currency, bank, and business document transferals.[130] The government willingly funded mail delivery as an essential economic component, and without federal mail contract support, sustainable western commerce would have been much more difficult than it already was, if not altogether impossible. Stage and freight companies depended on mail contracts for their survival.[131]

Stretching American civilization across the continent was anything but routine. Mail delivery remained a security issue throughout the nineteenth century. A report from a routine postal delivery of April 17, 1862 describes the daily hazards:

...passing from Split Rock Station west to Three Crossing of Sweet Water with the United States mails... (the mail party) was attacked by a band of Indians...resistance was made by said mail party for hours when the Indians retreated...six men out of the nine who

composed said party were wounded with arrows and five with guns.[132]

Following the established national security tradition, the twentieth century post assumed obligations that it alone among government institutions could meet.[133] In World War I, the postal establishment sold Liberty bonds and war savings certificates, registered enemy aliens, processed draft questionnaires, and recruited for the military.[134] It also implemented Congressional legislation to censor foreign mail and translate foreign government and war articles.[135] Thousands of postal clerks were shifted from domestic to military postal operations in direct support of the war.[136]

The World War II post assisted in alien address reporting, once again sold war bonds, issued civil service information, posted F.B.I. "wanted" posters, and located families of deceased servicemen. It also aided in new censorship activities, assisted in the apprehension of criminals, and recruited women for defense industry work. Most importantly, though, a completely interconnected domestic/military post exchanged "frequent and rapid communication with parents, associates, and other loved ones," and strengthened fortitude, enlivened patriotism, made loneliness endurable, and inspired "to even greater devotion the men and women who (carried) on the fight far from home and friends."[137]

A National Service Culture

While its history marks a place in national security, the post's culture describes why it could so capably serve contemporary homeland security interests. Postal culture has been shaped by the idea that delivery of mail is a committed public service instead of a purely

economic activity. The post's public service ideals
directly associate with the creation, growth, and protection of a nation.

Postal duty has always attracted citizens as an ide-
alistic pursuit that "gets into a man's blood" and "stays
there," according to depression era Postmaster General
James Farley.[138] American postal ideals were shaped
as early as the Pony Express, an institution that was
"special and they knew it...persist(ing) as though the
fate of a fledgling civilization rested in their hands - and
it did."[139]

The early postal symbol captures the cultural commitment to an aggressive, daring, committed pursuit
of service. Aptly described by David Brin's *Postman*
protagonist, Gordon Krantz: "the figure of a rider
(is) haunched forward on horseback before bulging
saddle bags, seeming to move at a flickering gallop."[140]
Backing the symbolism are storied slogans, such as one
repeated daily by nineteenth century postal legend, John
Butterfield: "Remember, boys, nothing on God's earth
must stop the U.S. Mail."[141] The unforgettable motto
adorning the main post office in New York City forever
reinforces the Butterfield mantra: "Neither snow nor
rain nor heat nor gloom of night stays these couriers
from the swift completion of their appointed rounds."

For over a century the most tangible manifestation
of this unique culture was "*service first*," a phrase that
became a way of life and ensured the safe and timely
delivery of mail, purchased as it was through the lives
of passionately committed public servants. Officially
adopted in 1851, Postmaster General Will Hays initially
floated *service first* in a speech thirty years earlier:

The postal establishment is not an institution for
profit, it is an institution for service...it is a great

human institution serving every individual in the country...300,000 men and women pledged to serve all the people...[142]

Congress backed the notion and carefully avoided a narrow business charter, when in the words of one postal chronicler, it could have but did not "provide only for the 'celerity, certainty, and security' of the mails..."[143]

Service first meant mail delivery and associated duties were expected to be secure and on time - *no matter what.* Whether riders in the west surmounting desert sands under a scorching sun, northern carriers churning through shoulder-high snowfalls, or mountain carriers stretching across narrow trails of the Sierra Nevada Mountains, the job would be done.[144] The mission on the front line, at remote mail stations, or in regional support facilities continued in the face of countless attacks - the fear of death notwithstanding - at the hands of highwaymen, Indians, robbers, lunatics, and others who would do harm to post or nation.[145]

As an obligation, *service first* could be met only through a relentless institutional pursuit of innovation and cooperation. Riders learned and employed a number of tactical evasions to protect their mail pouches, fend off or outrun the enemy, and keep lines of communication open.[146] Unconventional means were employed to connect near and far, even creating carrier delivery sleighs to cut through snow.[147] Working cooperatively with the U.S. Army, the post assisted in the mapping and use of military-cut trails to lead new roads into California.[148] Transportation and post collaboration ensured rural delivery in association with the Federal Highway Act of 1917, which opened travel all over the country and stimulated the interstate system.[149]

During the Indian Wars, the Army and the post implemented grain-feed (versus traditional grass-feed) for
postal horses, which both decreased delivery time and
provided a means of outrunning postal enemies.[150]

While *service first* is no longer formally advocated,
postal culture survives, albeit in a dormant state
relative to national security. In the words of 1990's
Postmaster General Marvin Runyon, "Our dedicated
men and women have never wavered in the pursuit of
their historic mission to deliver the mail. And we never
will."[151] The National Association of Letter Carriers
(AFL-CIO) reaffirms:

*We are career government employees who take
pride in our work, in our nation, and in the U.S. Postal
Service...letter carriers who deliver mail in the United
States are public servants who uphold their public
trust...*[152]

Dedicated today to customer service, efficiency, and
integrity, the traditional service obligation is advanced
through voluntary community activities such as feeding
the hungry, comforting children with grave illnesses,
caring for seniors, adopting schools, and sponsoring
blood drives. Annual food drives coordinated by the
National Association of Letter Carriers involve more
than 1,500 branches. Letter carriers participate as the
founding national fund raising sponsor for the Muscular
Dystrophy Association, having raised over $20 million
in the last 15 years of sponsorship.[153] These voluntary
and dedicated service activities hold the post's deep and
profound place as a national service culture.

The Post Office in the Contemporary National Establishment

Although defined by its public service commitment, the post's role in the national establishment has always generated differences of opinion. The dominant contemporary view aims for it to provide timely, affordable, secure mail service to all Americans. To accomplish these aims are reform debates that offer various combinations of the post's becoming completely privatized, an employee-owned company, a for-profit stock corporation, a subsidized public service in its historical form, or continuing as a government corporation.[154]

Privatization - or some form of it - dates throughout history, as witnessed in an argument made by Wells Fargo in 1864:

This part of business (i.e.: postal delivery) is very profitable, and its success, popularity and wide extension...present very effective practical arguments for the government's giving up wholly its post-office department...[155]

The privatization argument is made strictly on the basis of economy, and it is difficult to argue that a public entity - any public entity - can more effectively or efficiently deliver a purely economic service than could market-shaped organizations. Framed in a debate on these grounds, the Postal Service is (not surprisingly) losing the battle. Despite outsourcing many functions, the post scores low on most business indicators: labor runs approximately 80% of total costs;[156] capital spending is virtually frozen; debt is rising; and charges to customers have been adjusted up 8.7%.[157]

The terms of the debate need to change. Although efficiency is admirable, postal history clearly reveals societal value beyond the narrow definition of the bottom line. Rebalancing the role of the post in the national establishment to incorporate service on behalf of national interests would allow for the Postal Service to realize its contemporary societal potential.

Homeland Security Potential

Ideally structured for participation in homeland security, the Postal Service provides existing capabilities that require no additional investment and build on existing missions. Homeland security participation could also improve its core mail business. The capabilities include: (1) routinized work; (2) continental territorial coverage through decentralized letter carriers, post offices, and logistical support centers; (3) everyday/all day operations; (4) a crisis management-like command and control system that facilitates passing information and giving directives; (5) standardized motor vehicles and equipment (for installation of information technology and communications reporting systems); (6) internal (to the postal service) and external (for citizens) reporting processes; (7) training processes and infrastructure; (8) local, state, regional, and federal structure for coordination with other homeland security-focused organizations.

These capabilities lead to consideration of the Postal Service to significantly enhance existing homeland security programs or create new ones. Consideration in major areas is provided below.

Neighborhood Watch

Already a nationwide movement, the National Sheriff's Association estimates over 7,500 communities and 30 million people participate in grass roots neighborhood watch programs.[158] President Bush calls for a dramatic expansion of the concept with an antiterrorism focus added to the existing crime prevention mission.

Not counted in the National Sheriff's Association numbers or the President's expansion, the Postal Service runs the nation's largest conglomeration of neighborhood watches, consisting of a wide range of citizen watches, individual postal carrier assistance, and carrier alert programs. In citizen watches, neighbors exchange work and vacation schedules with trusted friends and neighbors to watch each other's mailboxes and homes. If a mail or home thief is at work, they call the local police and their postal inspector immediately.[159]

Carrier Alert, the most comprehensive postal watch, spans most every community in the United States. Focusing on elderly and handicapped citizens, the program was established in 1982 to provide assistance by perhaps the only point of human contact for some homebound patrons.[160] To enroll, the citizen fills out a form and receives a mailbox sticker to alert the letter carrier. Volunteering for such duty, letter carriers note anything unusual with member addresses and contact a social or health services agency.[161] Upon checking on the citizen, the partner agency then contacts the appropriate family, police, or emergency service.[162]

The Carrier Alert program's success is attributable to the network that has been formed among citizens, their next of kin, the Postal Service and National Association of Letter Carriers (AFL-CIO), and local sponsoring agencies such as the United Way, Red Cross, or Agency on Aging. While most of these organizations are national in scale, their work together is coordinated at the local level.

For homeland security, the post's neighborhood presence should be incorporated in the President's neighborhood watch expansion by involving citizens and their postal representatives in a terrorism reporting network. Using existing command and coordination channels run by local officials to higher authorities, a chain could work in the following fashion: local report from letter carrier to local neighborhood watch commander, to Citizen Corps Council and Postal Inspectors if necessary, and on to higher authorities as appropriate.

Information Technology Database Reporting

In addition to using an information reporting chain, incidents should also be entered by postal workers into a national level homeland security information system that would link postal reports with law enforcement and other sources into a searchable system. A database would provide a smartlink to seemingly isolated reports that could be tracked, analyzed for trends, and cross-referenced based on geography, name, crime, activity, and any other searchable characteristic.

To perform a related function among intelligence agencies, the President proposes a National Information System out of which an "Information Integration Office" has been proposed for use down to state and local levels.[163] Other national institutions mentioned in such a reporting system include the U.S. Coast Guard and the U.S. Merchant Marine Academy's Global Maritime and Transportation School, which provides training and "enhances the ability of mariners aboard American merchant vessels in inland waterways and the Great Lakes to track and record potential threats."[164] Also mentioned is a crime prevention program called "Highway Watch" among the American Truckers Association and six states.[165]

The National Information System needs to incorporate the previously mentioned Terrorist Information and Prevention System (TIPS) and a broadened reporting role beyond TIPS for the Postal Service. According to the original strategy, TIPS reporting would take place through a toll-free phone number. A phone number is insufficient to capture the many different reports that will come through an energized Postal Service and other communities that could be tapped as homeland security intelligence assets. To efficiently upload into a national system, postal employees need handheld and/or vehicle devices through which information can be entered and uploaded on the ground.

Leveraging postal and homeland security missions, the handheld device could serve multiple purposes and provide mail service efficiency as well. It should be integrated with former Postmaster General Runyon's information technology vision to "make our processing systems interoperable" through information technology tracking.[166] Handhelds are useful to blend hard copy and electronic communications, scan bar codes for package tracking, and track business reply cards with vital data and electronic status information.[167] One handheld device that plugs into a smart system can sit at the tip of a postal information, intelligence, and efficiency network.

Inspection

Dubbed as the post's "eyes and ears," postal inspectors are involved in every major aspect of criminal,

fraudulent, and negligent postal activity. Always se-
lected with care, this elite corps provides a mail security
reputation built on a coach and train heritage whereby
thieves purposely and carefully left the mail untouched,
knowing they would stand a much better chance to
escape with their bounty if they were outside of postal
jurisdiction.[168] Living up to its crack reputation through
modern times, these dedicated postal servants are the
linking pin through which postal homeland security
programs should run. Postal inspection should coordinate the post's homeland security agenda with other
organizations, disseminate information down to the
local postal employees, coordinate training for letter
carriers, and provide the intelligence filter needed to establish reporting standards, processes, and awareness.

Dissemination of Information

The greatest value of a democracy's postal system is
its unparalleled ability to disseminate information in a
digestible, sustainable, secure form for all citizens. As
postal delivery of newspapers began in 1792 to create
an informed citizenry out of frontiersmen, so should
today's mail be used as a primary means of homeland
security information dissemination by local, state, and
federal government. The post should be the primary
delivery vehicle of citizen preparedness, to include
distribution of a customized citizen homeland security
manual for every household. As an example of what
needs to come in much greater frequency, breadth, and
depth, the Washington, D.C. Emergency Management
Agency recently mailed all of its postal patrons a
"Family Preparedness Guide."[169]

Emergency Medical Service

Visiting every home and business throughout the United States, letter carriers encounter tragedy every day; they should be prepared to cope with it. Emergency medical training should be provided to every postal employee. Basic health crisis recognition and immediate health response services should be skills provided to all postal employees. In addition to the benefits of providing a beneficial public service, the training will acculturize the modern postal employee with the crisis management mindset necessary for homeland security contributions.

The post's tie to emergency medical service is a strong one. Recent acts of heroism exemplify the point. Letter carrier Michael Rudolph saved an 82-year old man who fell in his courtyard on a bitterly cold day and was found bleeding to death from a head wound. Rudolph stripped off his own shirt and applied it in a pressure grip to slow the bleeding, got medical attention for the victim, and saved his life.[170] Letter carrier Arthur Thim, having no experience with seizure victims, used common sense to save and care for a victim on his daily route until medical authorities arrived. Another carrier saw a heart attack unfold and was helpless to act other than to ask a neighbor to call 9-1-1. In a trained postal establishment these heroes' services should be expected occurrences rather than surprisingly heroic events.

Community Crisis Management and Pre-First Responder Preparedness

All postal employees should be trained to recognize, respond, and report gas, fire, smoke, and other physical disturbances to public and private structures as the first line of community defense. Isolated crisis management examples in this vein abound. Letter carrier John Curran smelled a gas odor on his mail route and immediately contacted his local utility to prevent a catastrophic leak from either intoxicating residents to death or exploding as an incendiary bomb in contact with flame.[171] Letter carrier Rickey Hebron was recognized for hearing a smoke alarm and alerting authorities to avoid a fire. Going a step further, Wanda Pugh observed a smoking building on her route and promptly ordered a day care center evacuation next door before a block of buildings went up in flames.[172]

Community crisis management should also involve the letter carrier's familiarity with consequence management fundamentals in response to a weapons of mass destruction attack. Should an attack occur, letter carriers will be on the scene even before weapons of mass destruction first responders arrive; therefore, they should be intimately familiar with the community's consequence management plan, to include immediate action responsibilities and first responder tactics. In short, letter carriers should know what assets will arrive behind them to manage the crisis. The carriers should be knowledgeable enough to assume a leadership role until the first responder community can mobilize, get on-scene, and take over command of the incident.

Anti-Terrorism Intelligence

Observed in the sought after post-September 11 intelligence capability, human assets on the ground provide a fundamentally different capability than do satellites and other remote sources. Serving as a domestic intelligence asset, all postal workers should be trained in the fundamentals of information gathering and reporting. Focused, not on intrusive methods that span far beyond their normal work duties or place them in compromising situations (or violate citizen Fourth Amendment rights), but on commonplace observations and basic analysis that can be obtained passively in the course of mail operations, postal employees should be trained to recognize and report suspicious activity.

Currently, the Postal Service is mentioned alongside other routinized workers as part of the proposed TIPS mission. The Postal Service should be afforded a special role beyond that given to truckers, cab drivers, and other professions. A trucker might be interested in volunteering for homeland security "eyes and ears" duties while on long stretches of interstate highway, but

---

Equipping the "Intelligent" Postal Employee as a Homeland Security Asset

1. **Communications**
   - Hand-held or vehicle-housed information reporting system uploads on-the-ground incident reports.

   - Voice communications system for crisis management incident reporting back to law enforcement, public health, fire and/or emergency medical authorities.

2. **Education and Training**
   - Anti-terrorism.
   - Intelligence 101.

3. **Emergency Preparedness**
   - Emergency medical training/CPR.
   - Community crisis management.
   - Consequence management/pre-first responder.

a Postal Service worker has an obligation to perform an age-old national security function. TIPS should specify intelligence roles for the postal service apart from other industries where public duty is not as engrained.

Procedures for paper- or information-based homeland security intelligence reporting, monitoring, and analysis are already in place. For example, mail theft is reported through "PS Form 2016, Mail Theft and Vandalism Complaint." By analyzing information collected from the form, Postal Inspectors may determine whether the problem is isolated or part of a larger mail theft problem.[173] A similar process should use these existing channels and enhance them through information technology database tracking and web input capabilities for reporting of terrorist threats.

Postal Terrorism Reporting Process

1. Terrorism-related observation made by a letter carrier trained to analyze fundamental anti-terroism intelligence situations.

2. On-the-ground hand-held (or vehicle-supported) electronic report uploaded for immediate distribution.

3. Electronic distribution into the National Information System database.

- Report is accessible to local law enforcement authorities.

- Report is accessible/searchable for federal intelligence use; it is integrated for trend analysis alongside other TIPS and intelligence reporting.

- If applicable, report is accessible by Postal Inspection Service.

Mail and Postal Facility Security

The post was, is, and most likely always will be a target. Its enemy appeal is in its ubiquitous public presence and universal recognition as an American symbol. Its personnel, products, and facilities provide a wide range of targeting potential both indirectly as a conduit to reach unknowing citizens and directly as a United States landmark institution. When looking for targets, the local post office will be a first choice for domestic terrorists, suicide bombers, or saboteurs.

A secure mail and secure mail facilities are crucial to the use of the mail as a means of regular communications, but in every generation, mail security is redefined. The post has responded to poisonous snakes in mail bags, highwaymen, robbers, Indians, mail bombers, and countless other threats in the past, and it will respond and protect against its present and future threats. Although postal workers suffered in recent Anthrax attacks in part due to a lack of information-focused package tracking capabilities,[174] the deployment of long awaited "intelligent" mail through bar code-like and other technologies is under development.[175] The post is also working to shore up the other end of the pathogen crisis - to establish detection and handling capabilities to prevent transferal through the mail.

In the future, research and development monies should be spent on identification and protection against the next great postal homeland security crises. Security management analysis should be conducted, and facility protection plans developed and implemented, for every major postal facility, much like they are conducted on diplomatic facilities overseas. Package tracking should also coordinate with postal intelligence reporting and postal inspection in the proposed National Information System.

Intergovernmental and Dual Use Initiatives

Representing perhaps the greatest homeland security lesson in postal history is the need for government, non-government, corporate, and voluntary organizations to work together in order to realize collective goals. First operating out of local taverns, [176] then floating under a captain's protection aboard merchant vessels for overseas transport, [177] then hitching clerks on mobile rail posts, [178] and even cooperating with Army student-pilots to provide cross country air training in exchange for intercontinental air mail, [179] the post understands how to work for mutual benefit among fellow public and private organizations.

Again leveraging service efficiency and homeland security, interorganizational cooperation is witnessed in the post's reading utility meters from postal vehicles as it navigates the community, collecting information for the power company as the mail is delivered, and reporting hazardous incidents to public safety organizations as previously mentioned.[180] Postal reporting for homeland security intelligence, participation in a national crime and terrorism neighborhood watch prevention program, and development of new capabilities to serve the public's health all dovetail as postal initiatives in support of other organizations.

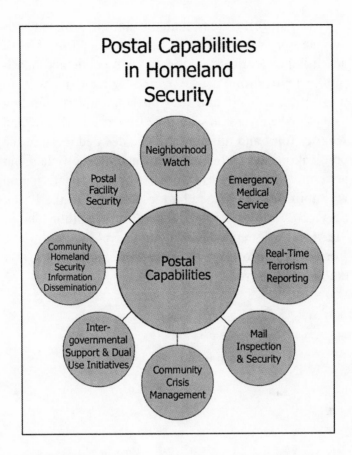

Conclusion

Throughout the 1990's and up to September 11, many public organizations hurtled towards economic efficiency, the Postal Service among them. Unlike post-September 11 adjustments in intelligence, law enforcement, transportation, public health, and military organizations, a comprehensive plan for postal homeland security has not emerged, and conventional wisdom still calls for "efficiency-only" mail delivery. Such thinking belies the post's contributions towards broader national interests.

It is painfully clear that the nation remains vulnerable to a wide number of homeland security threats,
and it is just as clear that the nation's public and quasi-
public institutions are expected to lead the way to
preventing them if humanly possible and responding
to them whenever and wherever they occur. Homeland
security roles and missions will be decided through the
political process by federal, state, and local officials, but
government's ability to lead the way to a secure nation
will ultimately be judged by the people. For the Postal
Service, "its future role," according to author Cheryl
McAfee, "will depend heavily on the role society wants
- or needs - it to play."[181]   Homeland security is a role
that must be played.

CHAPTER SIX

WHERE HAVE ALL THE COWBOYS GONE?[182] REINSERTING THE CITIZENRY IN AMERICAN SECURITY

Context

Homeland security is as much an attack from within as it is from without; a nation's homeland vulnerability reveals as much about its way of life as the concomitant professional prevention, mitigation, response, and recovery ways and means that result. While the United States government's emphasis on professionalizing the nation's homeland security through strategy, planning, and organization is an appropriate first step to a more secure homeland, the role of the citizenry must also be examined. The citizenry is not currently being considered as the central component of homeland security that it must become.

There are three types of citizen security commitment, with the first two listed below receiving major legislative attention and the third mostly forgotten in current planning (thus providing the purpose for this essay):

(1) National Service in government or government-sponsored programs such as the military, Americorps, Peace Corps, among others;
(2) Voluntary Service in formal full- or part-time programs such as work/study, "Citizen Corps Councils," "Senior Corps," the proposed Terrorism

Information and Prevention System (TIPS), among others;[183] and

(3) Citizen Service, which is vigilance as a characteristic of citizenship prior to, during, and after any number of homeland security situations.

The *national service* debate has been joined for years around the idea that an active societal obligation should be required of U.S. citizens. Post-September 11 homeland security application has sparked its renewal, which is aptly described by one observer as a "draft for the homefront." Others, such as President Bush, emphasize an increase in *voluntary service* programs old and new, with new administrative apparati to organize them.

What the debate misses is the fact that all citizens are not "joiners." Whereas a "draft" into national service signifies forced entry into professional ranks, more than just an enhancement of the nation's professional homeland security forces is needed. And, to volunteer is admirable, but for all citizens to feel the awesome weight of responsibility in protection of the nation as part of their own life is a different level of societal commitment.

Introduction

In the aftermath of September 11, the federal government has begun to address homeland security voids, such as transportation and immigration security; preparing the first national homeland security strategy; improving interagency coordination through executive department reorganization; and building intergovernmental capabilities through federal grants, state and local planning, public health assessments, and consequence management seminars.

As government develops its capabilities, the preparedness and participation of the citizenry stands in stark contrast. With the exception of President Bush's encouragement of military enlistment, increased participation in existing and new voluntary programs, and a since rejected Terrorist Information and Prevention System (TIPS) for certain groups to report suspected terrorist activities, the role of citizens has not been considered. Highlighting this inattention, a recent *Washington Post* editorial concluded the government has done nothing "concerning how (citizens) should prepare themselves and their homes for terrorist attacks...," an observation that reveals a missing but essential national priority - to place the citizen as a central actor in homeland security.

The citizen's role needs definition in order to provide a context for the homeland security generation to define itself in relation to its nation, similar to the founding generation's participation in the American Revolution or the World War II generation's myriad sacrifices home and abroad. The definition should include:

(1) Acknowledgment: recognition that this battleground's targets - *place* (where citizens live) and *people* (the citizenry itself) - cannot escape roles in the conflict and thus do not have the luxury of choice;

(2) Responsibility: reasonable, yet accountable citizen participation expectations;

(3) Tasks: practical self, home, and community tasks to be performed by citizens in all phases of homeland security; and

(4) Structure: a government-enabled network in which citizens and professionals learn of, train for, and participate in their respective areas of contribution.

As institutions, both government and citizenry face homeland security challenges. The government's twofold challenge is first to create and sustain professional organization for homeland security that encompasses all levels and functions to prepare for, respond to, and recover from homeland security contingencies; and second to facilitate participation of the citizenry in order to both maximize national homeland security capabilities and strengthen civil society in the process.

Citizen participation will be the most difficult aspect of homeland security to realize, a greater challenge than even government reorientation, reorganization, or intergovernmental coordination. Citizen participation alters two national security dynamics. First, while the government works *on behalf of* the citizens in most national security issues, it does not regularly work *with* the citizenry as a partner institution. The government typically functions as it has in the beginning of this homeland security effort, which is to encourage the citizenry to support government actions as a collective cheerleader, rally citizens to volunteer in or for government as part of the professional effort, or ask citizens to resiliently cope with the threat by carrying on life's work and leisure routines. Second, the citizenry is content with the roles government assigns - to be co-opted as volunteer or enlistee onto the professional side or to passively support from the sidelines. The citizenry shows little inclination to ask for, demand, or otherwise consider its unique potential contribution as a societal institution.

The Nature of the Threat: Why Homeland Security is Unique

The homeland security threat is distinguished by its unique "within and without" nature. Unlike a traditional domestic or foreign threat, the new breed of threat is a convergence of domestic and foreign. President Bush recognized this when he proclaimed, "the American people need to know that we're facing a different enemy than we have ever faced."[184] An example of this different enemy, the September 11 hijackers typify its dual-edged nature. They hid among the nation's citizens in plain sight, using American infrastructure, resources, training, weapons, and citizens to plan and carry out their attacks. Their tools included American visas, driver's licenses, credit cards, Internet access, automobiles, groceries, and libraries. No less than 19 of the hijackers resided for lengthy stretches as members of different small communities.[185]

This threat's second trait, which is significant but not unique, is the location of its impact: the United States. The U.S. Commission on National Security for the 21st Century ominously predicted: "Americans will likely die on American soil, possibly in large numbers."[186] The National Homeland Security Strategy reaffirmed the likelihood's permanency when it stated, "our society presents an almost infinite array of potential targets that can be attacked through a variety of methods."[187] When the impact is at home, different legal standards apply, it is America and Americans in harm's way as direct targets or collateral damage, and there is no psychological or physical separation of domestic resource mobilization "over here" and response operations "over there." American citizens, property, and mobilization and response resources are all targets; and, they will be for the foreseeable future.

A threat that is both within and without and impacts inside a nation's borders is interwoven in society. Described by historian Arnold Toynbee of societies bygone, interwoven enemy and regime-friendly alliances exerted pressures on ancient regimes. In physical terms, if external pressures outweighed regime stability, the regime would fall. Similarly, if internal force was in conflict with the regime, the greater force would prevail. Sometimes, an unsettling homeland equilibrium would be reached, in which combinations of internal/external and enemy/regime-friendly pressures would exert relatively equal force and throw society into uneasy turmoil.

The convergence of domestic and foreign, homeland as target and scale of its impact, and enemy domestic movement capability have not coalesced in such dramatically Toynbeen terms in the United States since large numbers of American colonists held firmly to and actively supported the Tory cause in the American Revolution. Just as in today's homeland security situation, the enemy threat came from within and without. America was the battleground; a way of life swung in the balance; colonists, the British Army, and foreign mercenaries formed the enemy; domestic resources served both sides; and enemy loyalties were hidden among the citizenry.

Toynbee's observations of an interwoven threat are contemporarily relevant wherein an enemy's ability to successfully organize from within and without to impact the United States is facilitated by the dynamics of modern society. A society that is organized less around agriculture and heavy industry and more around services and high technology is one that is increasingly more global and less local in orientation, mobile and less "rooted" in individual communities, and interconnected by professional or personal interests more than by physical place. Measuring one important outcome of this society by the decline of its "social capital," Harvard professor Robert Putnam concludes that Americans are less likely to know their neighbors in a meaningful way, participate in community associations, and volunteer. In more startling terms, the 1998 National Commission on Civic Renewal pointed to withering American civic life and concluded it a "nation of spectators."[188]

A loosening of the civic fabric that comprises American society enhances the threat under the first dictum of war - "know thy enemy." Any form of this new breed of enemy has momentary advantage in that it can know America and its citizens. Americans know less about each other within their communities and thus can less capably perceive internal disruptions in them, and American citizens as individuals know little, if anything, about the enemy.

The Government's Challenge

The government's great challenge is to not only organize and employ professional homeland security resources but to also recognize and act on the notion that the homeland will be much less secure without citizen involvement. As stated in the preamble to the Constitution, the federal government's role is to "provide *for* the common defense," which is different than *providing* a defense wholly on its own. Recognizing the distinction, a group of Harvard University weapons of mass destruction experts point out, "only a police state...could attempt to keep track of an entire society's movements, commerce, and private affairs."[189] Quite unlike a traditional military campaign on foreign soil, foreign campaign on American soil, or law enforcement imbroglio on any soil, the professional resources (i.e.: military, law enforcement, economic, diplomatic, intelligence, public health, emergency management) brought to bear by the government cannot wholly protect the nation and its people.

Also realizing that government cannot secure the homeland on its own, President Bush says "we must rally our entire society...,"[190] but acting on the realization is not as simple as it may seem. The government must first acknowledge its traditionally highhanded perception of civilians-in-defense, exemplified in the Cold War Civil Defense Commission's depiction of the citizenry as, "emotionally unstable, morally irresponsible, and corrupted by leisure, pleasure, and...commodity consumption." [191] Cold War research has since revealed that public apathy followed (not led as some have assumed) national leaders' disinterest in supporting a robust civil defense.[192] As a result, the citizenry neither received nor assumed a substantial role in that generation's homeland security.

While government rhetoric has changed, exclusion of the citizenry continues, even in areas of national security where citizen involvement should be unquestioned. For example, in wildland fire mitigation, "less than 1% of money spent has been used to educate homeowners about measures that they should take to reduce their vulnerability," despite the fact that fire science research shows the most effective defense against wildfire home prevention is to clear brush from the surrounding area and install fire-resistant roofs.[193] The solution, according to Forest Service scientist Jack Cohen, is "to have the private homeowner participate

in this problem."[194]   In a second example, the General
Accounting Office recently provided Congress with a
22-page list of recommendations on how to enhance
local preparedness for combating terrorism; every recommendation focused on what government could do to
more adequately prepare for and respond to terrorism;
no recommendation mentioned a citizen role.[195]   In a
final example, President Bush established five priorities
for the Office of Homeland Security: facilitate terrorism
information collection; coordinate the federal branch
for foreign intelligence gathering; coordinate nuclear,
chemical, and biological protocols; and disseminate
homeland security information among the federal
agencies.[196]   No priority addressed the citizenry, and
the President's follow-on initiative, the Department of
Homeland Security, provides no World War II Office of
Civilian Defense equivalent.

Putting the challenge in perspective, gov-
ernment-first national security thinking is a quite
appropriate reflection of society's division of labor.
The government provides a level of crisis management
effectiveness in every major national security issue that
citizen-participants could never achieve. Reliance on
professionals becomes a problem only when it fails
to incorporate the collective energies of a committed
people, which in turn undermines the civic foundations
upon which society is built. If evolved to an extreme
over several generations, civil capabilities atrophy if
not exercised; should citizens be called to employ them
in extremis, the capabilities are so foreign that they are
performed awkwardly, ineffectively, or not at all. In the
short term professionals may provide security, but the
citizen himself does not understand how or why that
is so. Lost are society's collective practical skills and
moral courage to withstand a crisis.

To avoid the extreme, the government's homeland security network must not only frame the roles and missions of its professionals but must also be an effective conduit for citizen participation. Facilitation of citizen participation must be handled adeptly or it will fail. Warning of the potential for citizen disinterest, a recent article in *Time* points out, "there's some risk... without a solid infrastructure to support them, the most avid volunteers will get frustrated."[197]

To be effective as a democratic republic's citizen conduit, government's ability to enhance citizen understanding of homeland security is primary and would be valuable purely for knowledge's sake, irrespective of its many other contributions. Homeland security is the twenty-first century's first litmus test of liberty, which in the words of John Adams, "cannot be preserved without a general knowledge among the people." Conversely, among an uniformed citizenry in events of great consequence, crisis management theorists see the potential for "xenophobia, vengeful fury, and other powerful forces" that could dramatically influence the nation's governance.[198] Just as any untrained, unknowledgeable person has difficulty dealing with the unknown, an unprepared citizenry is much more likely to experience dramatic social and psychological upheaval in the event of a serious homeland security situation. According to national security strategist, Chris Seiple, "the public's fear of the unknown is a top tier factor to overcome...knowledge is power."[199]

Knowledge may produce power, but among all national security issues, homeland security also uniquely invokes philosopher and mathematician Alfred North Whitehead's adage that "a merely well-informed man is the most useless bore on God's earth." How knowledge is transmitted and applied among the citizenry is also critical. The conduit must move information up and down, to and from the citizenry. One-way communication from Washington provides a much different message to the individual citizen than does two-way dialogue of citizens with local police departments, emergency management agencies, town councils, or local fire departments. Cabinet secretaries may inform of looming threats through national warnings or alerts, but security is tied to action, and action for the citizen only occurs at the local level. While the federal government must establish the framework, the local level must reassure its community by applying homeland security knowledge, wisdom, and know-how with citizens to produce planning, training, and operations unique to each respective community and people.

One example in which national security professionals frame citizen participation, but the facilitation role down to local levels must be improved, is in the U.S. Justice Department's, USA Freedom Corps', and National Crime Prevention Council's collaboratively published *United for a Stronger America: Citizens' Preparedness Guide.*[200] This guide categorizes citizen preparedness responsibilities in the home, work, and local community. Improvements must come when a framework such as this is: (1) recognized as important by every local community agency charged with citizen homeland security preparation, (2) the recognition is translated into action through a homeland security network that assists local officials in tailoring the framework to citizen responsibilities in each unique community, and (3) those local officials and their citizens can then apply the community responsibilities to every household's circumstances. As it stands now, the guide is not widely known as a resource, it is far too general to do much good without significant citizen investment in independent follow-on research, and it violates the very purpose for organizing federal homeland security resources under one department because it sends the well intentioned citizen through a Byzantine maze of no less than 18 different federal agencies.

Government is ultimately effective at those tasks for which it is uniquely structured. Providing a conduit for citizen participation in homeland security is one of those tasks. The mechanics of facilitation will be achieved if the appropriate end is in mind. The ideal end for government-facilitated participation is described by sociologist Severyn Bruyn:

> *Civilian defense...should be...the agenda for all nations that want to sustain a civil society... It cultivates moral and ethical character...(It) means the empowerment of ordinary people...teaching everyone how to combat terrorism with a sense of civic responsibility...teaching self-defense in the local community...building civic accountability...training citizens to deal with violence in mundane settings...not to add fear, but a sense of confidence in making a mature response to a real crisis...a broad educational method for developing a peaceful community life.*[201]

The Challenge to the Citizenry

The nation's leading military sociologist, Charles Moskos, believes "meeting the...threat will force us to confront our notion of citizenship,"[202] that notion redefining economic, recreation, and security roles. The citizenry must not only acknowledge that its commitment in a strong economic and republican foundation enables national security funding, organization, and authority, but must also accept that a strong social fabric with the citizen at its core is the source from which security is ultimately assured. Unfortunately, supporting the economic and republican foundation and building the strong social fabric are often viewed as paradoxical, one gained at the other's expense.

Exacerbating the challenge is the modern concept of leisure. In post-September 11 reflection, social scientist Thomas Massaro observes:

I suspect that many Americans are, like me, torn between two conflicting desires. On the one hand, we yearn for nothing more than the opportunity to revert to our comfortable pre-September 11 ways, even if some aspects of our culture and routines new seem a bit frivolous. On the other hand, we feel the steady pull of conscience, to move beyond business-as-usual and meet the recent challenges to our nation by reforming these same ways.[203]

Columnist Margaret Carlson describes the conundrum in stronger terms:

The first chance to turn the Selfish Generation into something more like the Greatest Generation was missed last fall when (President) Bush urged us to return to normalcy - at the mall, the cineplex and Disneyland.[204]

Between extreme models of "economic man," "leisure man," and "security man" is an appropriate role for the citizenry: continuing with life's work and leisure routines while altering the definition of what is routine. This balance is implicitly understood in the Office of Homeland Security, which recognizes, "we must balance the benefits of mitigating (terrorist) risk against both the economic costs and infringements on individual liberty that this mitigation entails."[205] Citizen routines must continue to contribute to the economy, account for recreation and leisure, and include social and spiritual well being, but they also must incorporate a role in homeland security.

An engaged citizen will contribute to two trends - "public building" and "civilian-based defense" - that enhance security and also reinforce civil society. Describing public building as consciously structured forums for people to work together as *citizens*, not just as *neighbors*, Kettering Foundation president David Mathews believes the people must encourage government to support community activism as much as government encourages the people. Only through citizens can "real change...happen at multiple levels, from the mayor's office to the neighborhood associations."[206] Public building not only provides direct benefits of awareness, intelligence, and preparedness (that are discussed later in this essay), but also enhances the general bonds of relationship, vigilance, and commitment among the citizenry - the bonds that form civil society. *Neighbors* building their public homeland security capability among one another as *citizens* form the beginnings of a "civilian-based defense."

To consider public building as a means to create a civilian-based homeland defense does not come easily; realizing such a notion requires real change in both thought and action, the two deep-seated habits that combine to form what is routine. Not only understanding homeland security's imperative but actively choosing and then sustaining the choice is both an emotional and rational citizen-decision:

People (in civilian-based defense) estimate the movement's potential effectiveness and the importance of their own contribution toward the group's success. If the perceived probability of movement success is low, people are less likely to participate. Even if success is more likely, if an individual's personal contribution is perceived as unimportant, participation will decline.[207]

Opting out has been the risky homeland security choice in recent history. Citizens - as a citizenry - have been as equally agreeable to cede their security responsibility to national security professionals as professionals have been willing to alone shoulder it. Although government did not encourage the public, Cold War research shows public apathy was the leading reason for that generation's lack of citizen preparedness. People associated scary "survivalism" with civil defense; they perceived a doomsday-like hopelessness of the cause; and they were uncomfortable in preparing because of the unpleasant thoughts conjured in doing so.[208] The citizenry must overcome homeland security's great misperception seen as common by activist Jane Goodall in seemingly intractable social issues:

You may be overcome...by feelings of helplessness. You are just one person...How can your actions make a difference? Best, you say, to leave it to decision makers. And so you do nothing.[209]

> "A valiant army has arisen, has gathered around Boston to contain the growing threat from the British soldiers there. But, in fact, it is not army at all. It is simply *us*. It is private citizens who recognize that no man in this continent has the luxury of sitting home surrounded by the comforts of family, while close by his own countrymen are denied that very comfort."
>
> - John Adams address to the Second Continental Congess.
>
> [in Jeff Shaara's *Rise to Rebellion* (p. 337.)]

A Concept for Citizen Engagement in Homeland Security

Having given "blood, their time, or their money,"[210] Attorney General John Ashcroft acknowledges the immediate citizen efforts in response to the attacks on the World Trade Center and Pentagon. As immediacy moves to long-term preparedness, new citizen responsibilities arise in prevention, mitigation, response, and recovery.

"Stop, Look, and Listen!": Citizen Prevention

Civicism. Citizen participation must be built by first addressing the overarching societal issues that make America an inviting target. General initiatives to promote civic activism lighten the homeland security burden, such as President Bush's leadership in promoting a reintroduction of rigorous civics curricula in schools, energizing citizens by calling on them to volunteer *at something* on behalf of society, and linking churches into secular outreach through faith-based initiatives.

A more active definition of citizenship specifically in homeland security will address the indirect refuge that an unaware citizenry provides enemies in American communities. As part of civicism's renewal, a comprehensive *homeland security citizen preparedness education program* should be facilitated from the federal level but tailored and delivered at the local level in schools' civics curriculum for children and in local communities' town councils, workshops, and neighborhood associations for adults. Local programs and leadership to achieve national understanding is the only way to build homeland security through citizens who know one another, watch out for one another and the community, and individually and collectively prepare every home, work, and community against potential threats.

Citizen Intelligence. The importance of the citizenry as an intelligence asset cannot be understated. It is "the heart of prevention" according to John Calhoun, the President of the National Crime Prevention Council: "watch(ing) out and help(ing) out...reporting...and contributing."[211] This importance must be reflected in every local community's homeland security plan and incorporated into the national homeland security strategy. Citizen intelligence cannot be reduced to a fraction of volunteers from select groups reporting through the Terrorist Information and Prevention System (TIPS).

As part of the government's role in facilitating citizen participation, local homeland security professionals should educate and train citizens in basic intelligence collection methods through classes, literature, and town hall meetings. The type of intelligence the citizenry can

assist with is much of what is also expected of local law
enforcement:

- "What and who are we looking for?"
- "What questions should be asked to gain information,
  if any, before reporting the issue to authorities?"
- "What kind of information should be passed to the
  federal level for analysis?"[212]

Any information gained from the citizenry should
be analyzed locally, and where appropriate, it should
be transmitted through the government's homeland
security information network for trend analysis and integration with broader national and international signs
of suspicious activity. Doing so would enable the detailed analysis necessary to uncover, locate, and stop
any new breed terrorist threat before it is realized.

Citizen intelligence should not be misconstrued as a
"snitch" system whereby neighbors report on innocent
neighbors. Part of redesigning the nation's intelligence
system must include a strengthened focus on civil liberties' protection. Frivolous claims must be sorted from
valuable information. Malicious false information must
be punished under the law, its product destroyed at first
reporting without circulation. Media leaks involving
citizen intelligence must not be tolerated in any way.

"You Gotta Believe!": Citizen Mitigation

The downfall of mitigatory efforts in the 1970's was
due largely to "engendered resignation" that "long-term
survival following an atomic war was neither possible
nor particularly desirable." [213] Unfortunately, waiting
and only then reacting, "even with extremely effective
consequence management efforts," according to crisis

management expert Michael Dobbs, "can do little more than mitigate the suffering of those afflicted."[214] To take mitigation seriously, the government must convey to the citizenry, and the citizenry must believe, that long-term survival can be achieved after either a singly devastating homeland security incident or a long-term campaign. Believing - by government and citizenry - is the key to sound government-facilitated pre-crisis preparation.

The citizen's first mitigation responsibility is the preparedness of him- or herself, the family, and private property. The government's role is to assist the citizen in that preparedness. Building disaster-resistant homes and communities is something that most citizens (outside of those that regularly deal with violent natural disasters on an annual basis) know little or nothing about, but there are many models of government-facilitated citizen preparedness that could change this situation. For example, the Federal Emergency Management Agency (FEMA) has worked successfully to instill disaster-prevention principles and translate them with local citizens and contractors into prevention measures at the community level.[215] The Home Front Command of the Israel Defense Force coordinates the distribution of gas masks, ensures all new homes are built with a protective space or room, and assists citizens in their homeland security preparations.[216] Other examples include:

(1) *Wildfire Risk* - using landscaping to create a buffer zone by pruning branches at 8-10 feet; removing debris from gutters;

(2) *Hurricane Risk* - installing storm shutters on windows; reinforcing roofs with hurricane straps and bracing;

(3) Earthquake Risk - anchoring bookcases; fastening shelves to walls; securing heavy furniture; purchasing earthquake insurance;
(4) Flood Risk - elevating main breaker and central electric equipment; purchasing flood insurance; and
(5) Nuclear Risk - securing a room in the home or sharing a common room among neighbors with basic short-term safety survival needs.

A full-scale citizen plan should be tailored to the unique situation of every residence in every different community. The plan should include biological, radiological, chemical, and traditional threat contingencies, since each threat requires a different response. Built into the plan should be the common and unique characteristics associated with major citizen responsibilities:

- *Infrastructure Protection*: although considered the province of "survivalist nuts," fallout shelters were designed in the 1960's with applicable intentions today - "to help people survive...and remain protected for several days...stocked with food, water, medical equipment, and...monitoring devices."[217]
- *Household Management*: a household checklist.
- *Health Care*: disaster first aid capabilities and resources; symptoms checks and emergency actions against the most likely biological, chemical or nuclear agents.
- *Child Care*: a school checklist for children.
- *Evacuation*: specific plans on how to escape from a contaminated community to a safer environment (i.e.: a travel checklist, where to meet, where to go, multiple routes of egress, etc.),
- *Communications*: all homes should possess a communications plan complete with emergency phone

contacts, alternate communications plans, and emergency community services.

"The Man with the Plan": Citizen Planning

Once self, family, and private property mitigation are integrated into citizen preparedness, the citizen must know his or her community role. Unfortunately, local governments and citizens are generally as unplanned as Pennsylvania's were prior to Three Mile Island's 1979 nuclear scare, when there were a "total lack of detailed plans in the local communities."[218] Three Mile Island's warning still offers profound citizen planning advice today:

Planning can be conceived...as a social process... that includes the establishment of viable channels for communication and interaction between...local, state, and federal agencies...(and) involves the interface of various units in the development, testing, and updating of written plans...it involves educating the public and developing a public understanding of potential hazards and appropriate protection action...Planning for incidents...should not be divorced from the day-to-day planning activities of the community. If planning is normalized...made a part of daily life and organizational activity, then an emergency is not a disjointed, abrupt departure from everyday life.[219]

Local government's planning responsibility includes ensuring that its manpower and resources and state and federal support are integrated with citizen roles into a coherent plan that all parties understand. Citizen volunteers will most certainly be needed to fulfill specific roles; such roles must be identified in the local community's homeland security plan. Citizens must learn their role in the plan, practice it during scheduled times, and be prepared to implement it on a moment's notice.

"I am Ready, Willing, and Able": Citizen Response

In the event of a homeland security catastrophe, citizens will most likely be the first on-scene, even prior to first responders. As stated in a recent article in the *Journal of Homeland Security*, "self-help will largely be the rule for many citizens during the initial hours of a large-scale...incident."[220] The most likely citizens on-scene include those with normal routines that place them in public places, such as utility crews, letter carriers, meter readers, transportation crews, public works employees, and neighborhood watch volunteers, among others.

According to law enforcement specialists, Paul Maniscalco and Hank Christen, the first citizen response principle is *scene awareness*,[221] the only stage in a consequence management incident in which professionals may not be involved with the citizenry as part of the response. Scene awareness is understanding the surroundings, significance, history, and other significant information that might assist in the response. It is the part of a response that the citizenry could be most uniquely qualified to assess, particularly if the scene is to be viewed in the broadest definition of the term, such as the nuances of a neighborhood or borough that only a resident would know, in order to avoid a narrow tactical orientation taken by most professionals.

Scene control is also a part of a homeland security response in which the citizen role is crucial.[222] Until first responders arrive, it will be citizens directing, collaborating, and working among each other to safety. Even after first responder arrival, it will be citizens who must remain calm, follow procedures, and assist with the response. A knowledgeable, trained citizenry will be much more capable of controlling emotions and actively becoming part of the solution instead of passively being part of the problem - a response instrument instead of a helpless target. Citizens must be trained to contact follow-on responders, identify early victims, witnesses, or assailants; avoid triggering secondary devices designed to impact once a crowd has gathered; and avoid contaminating a scene for evidence and/or the spread of infectious substances.

> "The men had drilled and planned for this moment for many months, and now they dressed in the dark as their wives pulled together a knapsack, a bit of food perhaps, bread or dried meat, laid out on the table beside a powder horn. It took barely a minute, and with a last soft word, the men were out of their houses, moving into the road, following the tracks of the horseman who woke them, knowing only the tracks that led to Lexington."
>
> - Paul Revere's observations on his historic ride to warn of the British advance on Lexington, Massachusetts.
>
> [in Jeff Shaara's *Rise to Rebellion* (p. 290.)]

"This Too Shall Pass": Citizen Recovery

Recovery is both literally and figuratively miscon-
ceived as an afterthought in most management of crises,
but its psychological impact drives every other phase of
citizen homeland security participation. With society's
physical, moral, psychological, and public health tested
during and after events of great consequence, every
citizen must understand in times of peace that tragedy
will inevitably strike. If citizens know that all national
energies, including their own, will be focused on a
healthy recovery, then hope will influence all of the
many actions necessary to achieve true homeland security.

American citizens have no difficulty in grasping
their various roles to assist their fellow citizens, community, and nation in traditional efforts to "return to
normalcy" in the wake of events of great consequence.
But, recovery is more than actions in the aftermath; it
is a continuous strategy that begins with the last crisis
and translates those lessons into capabilities needed in
the next crisis. Citizens must be put in a position to
apply the knowledge gained in being a target on the
Cold War's 40-year nuclear edge, living through the
Three Mile Island scare, and rebuilding in the wake of
the Oklahoma City bombing and World Trade Center
attacks. Crisis management theory suggests as much:
"we must make adjustments...after a crisis has occurred
in our network or elsewhere...we study it for ways to
improve upon our own efforts."[223]

Conclusion

The short-term citizen response to the attacks on the World Trade Center, Pentagon, and various mail facilities and recipients has been one of unquestionable support. As the short term moves out of the collective psyche; however, the inevitable urge to ignore the lessons of September 11 has crept into the national conscience, expressed by journalist Michael Kinsley in his views on "How to Live a Rational Life":

...a more rational approach to protecting ourselves from terrorism may not be doing more about it, or doing something different, but actually doing less. We need the courage and good sense to bury our heads in the sand a bit.[224]

As much as citizens want to "reimagine the past to make it more coherent, meaningful, (and) bearable"[225] as trauma psychologists say humans instinctively do, American citizens must not fictionalize their obligations as a societal institution. Homeland security is a war - the people's war - and war's principles apply, among those that of the *moral factor* that weighs a society's willingness to recognize conflict for what it is and support it with all necessary means. In homeland security, where the citizen is at once both target and combatant, the support of the American citizenry as an institution must at once reaffirm its democratic republican ideals and back up that commitment by working with government as a sustained instrument of national power. Citizens must both practically assist in securing the homeland and feel the sense of security within themselves for having been part of the effort.

"Doctor, I am not so sure about this. I am afraid that I am but an amateur in these affairs."

Franklin put a hand on his shoulder, and Adams heard the old man say with a laugh,

"So are we all, Colonel. So are we all."

- George Washington to Benjamin Franklin moments after Washington was voted Commander of the Continental Army by the Second Continental Congress.

[in Jeff Shaara's *Rise to Rebellion* (p. 340.)]

CHAPTER SEVEN

THREE MILE ISLAND - THE 20TH CENTURY'S INTRODUCTION TO THE 21ST CENTURY CRISIS

By Chris Seiple and Michael Hillyard

"I survived Three Mile Island...I think."[226]

Capsule

Three Mile Island has been as thoroughly examined as any crisis in history. This paper seeks not to recount events that have been told in other settings; rather, it uses those events to form conceptual lessons where humanity and science intersect in other complex systems. Although other systems share the crisis potential of "a Three Mile Island," many unknowingly violate its hard-earned wisdom. One such system is the United States preparedness and response for and to weapons of mass destruction terrorism. The relevance of Three Mile Island is addressed for this system so many years "after the fact."

The Modern Crisis

A growing number of theorists who study risk purport modernization as society's root cause of disaster. They believe modernization submits the human race to today's "era of disasters" and stands it on the "brink of self-annihilation."[227] This notion of end times is predicated on the assumption that technological and scientific risks and their associated consequences are not adequately considered in complex systems that combine technology, science, and the human condition. In such systems it is not a matter of "if" but "when" they will go wrong, and when they do, the chance for shockingly large consequences is high.[228]

What is it about the destructive potential of modern science and technology that leads rational thinkers to consider the end of the known world? What sets modern crises apart from catastrophes that have afflicted mankind since an errant camp flame sparked the first wildfire across an open field - or in more modern times, the first industrial blast furnace combusted in the face of an unlucky swing shift? In order to understand the answers to these questions, it is important to go to the source when they should have been raised: before, during, and after six frightening days in 1979.

Nuclear power gave birth to the modern crisis. Its potential downside was not objectively considered until it was almost too late. Even though the nation had been of nuclear age for a quarter century, and in that time operator and technical errors had already formed seven major radiological problems,[229] the abject uncertainty and potential horror of modern science, engineering, and management first coalesced in the public eye at Three Mile Island. Once the troubles in central Pennsylvania began, the questions came too fast, and subsequently, the answers were a rush to judgment. The first modern crisis was upon a community, industry, and nation.

The heart of Three Mile Island was its abstract nature. Energy, radiology, physics, and biology - once perceived as the benign outgrowths of never-ending progress - confusingly violated the public consciousness. Millirems, potassium iodate, meltdown, "going solid," and "half-life" alarmingly entered the national lexicon. The shepherds of progress - scientists, engineers, and technicians - who by their very nature avoided spectacle and circumstance, were thrust into the stream of mass communications, neither science nor public ready for interactive roles together. Although the nation did not wish to comprehend the nuclear dangers it faced, Three Mile Island forced a confrontation with reality through its many potentially consequential discrete issues, and more importantly, those issues' unknowable combination into an exponential threat. The issues proved completely beyond the grasp, and for that matter, the vision and every other sense of the American people.

Three Mile Island's organizational requirements caught the nation, in the words of a local mayor, "with our pants down." If pants were in fact down, they had gotten there through decades of collective ignorance and incompetence of regulators, operators, politicians, managers, scientists, technicians, and engineers. The issues of Three Mile Island in no way complied with the irrelevant collection of policies and procedures of governing jurisdictions and agencies; they swept away the ignorant and comforting misperceptions of an unwitting local citizenry; they disabused the industrial mythology of modern science's infallible safety; and they overwhelmed government's eroded disaster capabilities that were created for a different threat in a different era. The uncertainty of Three Mile Island's circumstances called for no mere fire, police, military, or medical response. By default, the response to those circumstances became an ad hoc assemblage of local and state *emergency and civil defense managers*; *federal regulators* in Washington, Philadelphia, and on-site; *political oversight* from the President of the

United States, Governor of Pennsylvania, congressional and state legislative members, mayors, and county commissioners; *scientific analysis* from environmental activists, physicists, and academics; *public health advice* from local doctors, radiation theorists, and state and national public health officers; *crisis management* at the plant itself by on-staff operators, their corporate experts, and the plant's designer; and *public relations* by the plant operators and every level and function of government.

Luckily, the result of such unpreparedness was little more than shock, embarrassment, and many good lessons to be learned. Unfortunately, the most valuable lesson has yet to be learned. Three Mile Island has been mislabeled an "accident," its subsequent application constrained within the narrow confines of the nuclear industry. It did, however, establish a recognizable pattern for systems wholly unrelated to it as destructive combinations of people, technology, and science with consequences so potentially horrific that when they occur, no one is quite sure what is wrong, what should be done, or what will happen next.

In Three Mile Island - and in the modern crisis - *the consequences are the crisis.* In relation to the three generation human life span (which includes consideration of one's children and grandchildren), the potential consequences of "a Three Mile Island" are forever. And dealing with "forever" is the job of an entire society, as Chernobyl demonstrates, because no one entity, public or private, can do it alone. While other modern crises may or may not take on the "invisible" aspects of radiation that so complicated the preparation, response, and recovery for Three Mile Island, they all ripple through society with long term consequences, possessed as they are with potentially destructive combinations of people, technology, and science. Some forever alter financial markets. Others uproot the political stability of a country or region. Still others dramatically alter industry. Below is Three Mile Island within the context of modern crises:

Crisis	Type	Year
Windscale Reactor Radioactive Release (England)	Nuclear	1957
Idaho Falls Federal Reactor Kills Three Workers	Nuclea	1961
Enrico Fermi Reactor Core Meltdown	Nuclear	1966
Lucens Vad Reactor Radiation Release (Switzerland)	Nuclear	1969
Brown's Ferry Reactor Dangerous Cooling Water Level	Nuclear	1975
Three Mile Island	**Nuclear**	**1979**
Tennessee Valley Authority Sequoyah 1 Plant Coolant Leak	Nuclear	1981
Tsurga Plant Radiation Exposure During Repairs (Japan)	Nuclear	1981
Tylenol Poisonings	Chemical/Terrorism	1982
Lebanon Suicide Bombings	Political/Terrorism	1983
Bhopal/Union Carbide Disaster	Nuclear	1984
Air India Flight 182 Bombing	Political/Terrorism	1985
Nuclear Cylinder Burst after Improper Heating	Nuclear	1986
Challenger Space Shuttle Explosion	Industrial	1986
Chernobyl Radiation Release	Nuclear	1986
Mad Cow Disease	Biological	1986 - Present
Pan Am Flight 103 Crash	Industrial	1988
Chilean Grape Cyanide Scare	Chemical	1989
Exxon Valdez Oil Spill	Industrial	1989
Los Angeles Riots	Revolt	1992
Branch Davidian Compound Raid	Law Enforcement	1993
World Trade Center Bombing	Terrorism	1993
Syringes in Pepsi Cans	Terrorism	1993
Somalia Attack	Military	1993
Orange County Financial Collapse	Financial	1994
Earthquake in Kobe, Japan	Natural	1995
Tokyo Sarin Gas Attacks	Chemical	1995
Collapse of Barings Bank	Financial	1995
Oklahoma City Bombing	Terrorism	1995
Nazi Victims Gold in Swiss Banks	Financial	1996 - 1998
Crash of ValueJet Flight 592	Industrial	1996
Crash of TWA Flight 800	Industrial	1996
U.S. Army Female Recruit Sexual Harassment	Legal	1997
U.S. Embassy Attacks in Kenya and Tanzania	Terrorism	1998
Tokaimura Processing Facility Uranium Container Overload	Nuclear	1999
Columbine High School Shootings	Traditional	1999
Earthquake in Turkey	Natural	1999
LAPD Ramparts Corruption Scandal	Legal	1999
Ford/Firestone Tire Crisis	Industrial	2000

Concorde Crash	*Industrial*	*2000*
USS Cole Attack	*Terrorism*	*2000*
Earthquake in India	*Natural*	*2001*
California Energy Crisis	*Energy*	*2001*
World Trade Center/Pentagon Attacks	*Terrorism*	*2001*
Anthrax Mailings	*Biological/Terrorism*	*2001*
Enron, Anderson Collapses	*Financial/Legal*	*2001 - 2002*

(Compiled from lists originally created by crisis management expert, Ian Mitroff and the 2002 World Almanac of Facts)

If this list of crises extrapolates into the future, that future will produce many and varied more. Some crises require no predictive imagination at all. For example, the Leningrad Nuclear Power Plant, a contemporary ticking time bomb within Three Mile Island's very industry, currently exposes 70-feet long, 8-inch wide cracks in its radioactive storage cement facility. Its reactor containment room pegged "off the scale" in a recent radiation measurement.[230] The heart of its workforce - Russian nuclear technicians - receives their pay as much as six months late.[231]

There is hope, however, that the future can be brighter than the recent past. Modern science and technology can be harnessed, controlled, and managed to safely achieve humane ends; in fact, this is the case in many complex systems today. To even begin to consider how this is so, one must first ask: "why do crises happen?" If this question is to be asked, it must be objectively considered. There are two dominant explanations that lead to its answer. The first focuses on the human condition and assigns "operator error" (in its most general sense) as the root cause of crises. Negligence, lack of attention to normal operations (i.e.: preventive and routine maintenance, shortcuts, etc.), misplaced priorities (i.e.: profit seeking versus safety, inappropriate or lack of regulatory compliance standards, etc.), unrealistic confidence in abilities to control risk,[232] and purposeful destruction or exploitation are all examples of the human condition in crises. The causal factor is human if three conditions are met:

(1) Something happened that could have been prevented by a person or persons;
(2) The person or persons had a moral obligation to undertake necessary measures to prevent the problem; and
(3) They could have taken those measures and had no legitimate reason for not doing so.[233]

The second explanation assigns blame to system complexity. Its underlying assumption is that humans have created systems of science and technology so complicated they are incapable of anticipating every potential outcome, managing the complicated designs and tight interrelations of those systems, or capably responding to problems inherent in either of the first issues in a manner that resolves them without substantial consequences. In system complexity theory, failures are inevitable.[234]

While system complexity raises the chances and stakes of disaster, recent history's many crises and the tragic "Leningrads" of the near future refute the fatalistic notion that posits crises as natural, inevitable, and unstoppable byproducts of modern society. Events that make "the list" are crises precisely because something went wrong to prevent an event from occurring, process from unfolding, or system from being built or operating to appropriate standards. Or, once the unexpected occurred, the system was not appropriately designed to withstand its own consequences, failed (or was not prepared) to adequately respond to them, or lacked the capacity to recover from them. *The consequences are the crisis.*

This essay presents Three Mile Island as a complex system of human designs, operations, response, and recovery. All systems possess human intervention, and all humans bring the human condition into their systems - all of their strengths, weaknesses, jealousies, fears, education, training, experiences, habits, and inattentions.[235] Human beings and their institutions - one or in combination - are ultimately responsible for the success or failure of a system. Award winning journalist Mark Stephens provides a Three Mile Island example of this point, when he rhetorically asks, "Faulty pipes, valves and instruments can be repaired or replaced, but is there a repair for reckless self-interest?"[236] His Three Mile Island thesis is distinguished by its focus on the human causes behind the first modern crisis:

> *Rather than supporting or condemning an energy source, the book looks at people, agencies, institutions, and ideologies interacting against the backdrop of a particular technology.*[237]

Once the human role is understood, then ways of addressing it can follow. To prevent, mitigate, respond to, and recover from crises, one must find amazingly secure systems. People in such systems constantly and continuously analyze "what could happen," "why might it happen," and "why could it be permitted to occur?" They then ask, "regardless of pre-crisis analysis, the unexpected happened...now what?" Addressing the questions and answers leads to the crisis management cycle of prevention, mitigation, planning, response, recovery, and wisdom. Studies of high-reliability organizations that continuously go through this process reveal the following characteristics:

(1) High levels of technical competence and sustained performance;
(2) Regular training;
(3) Structured redundancy;
(4) Collegial, decentralized authority patterns;
(5) Processes that reward error discovery and creativity;
(6) Adequate and reliable funding;
(7) High mission valence;
(8) Reliable and timely information; and
(9) Protection from external interference in operations.[238]

"Only luck saved the people around Three Mile Island. But we can't continue to rely on luck."

- Mark Stephens,

Three Mile Island: The Hour-by-Hour Account of What Really Happened

---

Three Mile Island and Weapons of Mass Destruction Terrorism

In Three Mile Island, America possesses its only experience managing the consequences of an incident truly capable of mass destruction. After all was said and done, a local couple unknowingly provided its wisdom, when they noticed "the typical reporter...was not prepared to interpret this type of [incident], where no death or injury, no fire, water, or visible wreckage was

involved."[239] That couple was speaking of the media but
to the nation. No one was "prepared" because nothing
like it had ever happened before. To compound the
problem, the threat itself - radiation - was invisible. Not
only was it invisible, but so was its effect. Visible evidence might not have appeared for years as radiation ran
its course through the bodies of community members,
livestock, plants, and waterways. The long term psychological trauma in the community and across the country
would also have been hard to visualize.

Lacking visible evidence, there was no tangible
proof of a crisis. The only physical evidence was
government and media reporting. Even the plant itself
looked normal. As a result of its intangible nature,
Three Mile Island became an event of perception and
interpretation. Such an event is scary, because the
threat is masked and therefore feeds on the most fundamental of human fears - the unknown. Whereas war
displays its horrid carnage and tornadoes pave swaths
of destruction, distortions of chemistry, radiology, or
biology add a completely new dimension to a crisis.
The unknown is handled only through the exchange of
information - information that is accurate, relevant, and
deliverable to and from those who know to those who
need to know it in order to resolve the crisis. The case
of Three Mile Island tells quite a bit about this type of
exchange. It had never happened before and was never
envisioned to take place; therefore, it was not planned,
and as a result, many mistakes were made. Events were
wrongly interpreted and poor assumptions led to faulty
judgments that put a nation at risk.

Change the dateline and subject, but keep the fear
and uncertainty, and therein lies the contemporary discussion of another issue at the convergence of science,
misguided intentions, management, and politics: how

to manage the consequences of weapons of mass destruction terrorism. If Three Mile Island was bad, weapons of mass destruction is worse. At Three Mile Island the threat was the radiation itself; weapons of mass destruction shares the consequences but adds the motives. Terrorists must be traced to foreign lands or domestic addresses. They may represent a rogue nation or have no "return address" at all. If they operate like many modern terrorists, there may be no opportunity to negotiate. Even more frightening is the fact that an end to terror may not be knowable. Local, state, and federal government will be in crisis. Time will be short. Decisions will have to be made. Force might have to be applied. An enemy will have to be pursued. Despite these dramatic complications, the heart of weapons of mass destruction terrorism and Three Mile Island is the same - the unknown - and it must be handled through the exchange of information.

What Threat, What Consequences?

The nation's "caught with our pants down" pre-Three Mile Island nuclear preparedness mirrored pre-September 11 weapons of mass destruction terrorism preparedness. The sense of false security - that a threat may not exist - was the same, as witnessed in the General Accounting Office's 1999 estimation of a weapons of mass destruction attack:

In most cases terrorists would have to overcome significant technical and operational challenges to successfully make and release chemical or biological agents of sufficient quality and quantity to kill or injure large numbers of people...[240]

In September 11's aftermath, despite a flurry of homeland security rhetoric and legislative proposals, not much has changed, as indicated by a homeland security task force report:

America remains dangerously unprepared to prevent and respond to a catastrophic terrorist attack on U.S. soil...in all likelihood, the next attack will result in even greater casualties and widespread disruption to American lives and the economy.[241]

The threat was and is real. Even if Tokyo's 1995 sarin gas attack was the world's only evidence, it proves these events will occur. Even if the former Soviet Union's missing nuclear materials were the only untraceable potential weapons of mass destruction, they would be enough. But such documented data points do not tell the entire story; they are supported by significant research. Among others, Harvard's Richard Falkenrath concludes, "the risk of a covert NBC (Nuclear, Biological, Chemical) attack against the United States is rising...and...at present is seriously underestimated by U.S. leaders and officials."[242] The recipe for concocting "the biological equivalent of an atomic bomb," according to bioterrorism expert, Richard Preston, "is no secret."[243]

While the threat is real, there are likely and unlikely forms weapons of mass destruction can take, each with different consequences. Focusing on the nuclear terrorism threat that aligns most directly with Three Mile Island's consequences, conventional wisdom dictates preparedness for weapons of mass destruction focused less on nuclear exchange and more on one-time tactical incidents. As summarized recently in the *American Spectator*, "no one believes that we face the threat of an all-out nuclear exchange."[244] A distinguished group of national security experts recently concluded, "Terrorists may acquire a weapon of mass destruction, but they will not have unlimited access to these weapons."[245] The most looming threats involve one of the following circumstances:

(1) Use of a non-nuclear device to achieve a nuclear reaction;
(2) Clandestine entry into a nuclear facility to turn a nuclear facility's power against itself; or
(3) Use of a small nuclear device to achieve some combination of a primary explosive and secondary radiation effect.

The non-nuclear device strategy provides many options for the assailant and should be carefully considered. Its most obvious employment is a repeat of September 11's transportation-delivered payload. A plane crash, for example, would likely result in a major radiation release and a significant loss of nuclear coolant.[246] The immediate consequences of this type of one time event, even if it were to occur, are imminently survivable if the collective nuclear network of industry, plant, emergency management, public health, and safety is prepared.

Industry insiders know that such preparation is a long way off. For example, nuclear power plants have not been designed to withstand sabotage, even though the post-September 11 nuclear industry has paid careful attention to its woeful physical security in existing plants and is altering designs for new plants. Gaping holes remain. For example, the nation's 26 university research reactors are "a big problem" according to arms control expert, George Bunn, because "research reactors are much closer to city populations," they have not been as closely design-regulated as power plants, and they have no external protection against sabotage.[247]

Turning the power of a nuclear facility on itself to create a weapon of mass destruction is another issue. The potential for this means of destruction can be measured in two ways: the potential to access the facility and the potential to destructively exploit such access. Regarding the access issue, numerous breakdowns in plant security have led to criminals being granted access to sensitive areas. Plant inspectors routinely find inoperable alarms and video surveillance cameras, guards who are not trained in their weaponry, and faulty guns.[248] Terrorist-simulated exercises conclude with "red teams" penetrating the control room (even after giving advanced notice of their strike).[249] The previously mentioned university reactors present a security challenge as well, their freewheeling institutional culture likened by one analyst to the "Keystone Cops."[250]

In addition to plant design and security is a failure to recognize the complete nuclear target, for many threats fall outside of physical plant confines. For example, nuclear waste sites have traditionally gone un- or under-protected, yet they are as vulnerable as the plants. The waste pool, for example, can be a more dire threat than a meltdown of the fortified reactor core.[251] At Jordan Lake's North Carolina Shearon Harris Nuclear Plant, where spent fuel assemblies are stored, terrorism-induced water loss to its waste pool could trigger tremendous human losses and according to one analysis, "render an area the size of North Carolina un-inhabitable..."[252]

A third form of nuclear employment is the use of a tactical weapon. The potential destruction varies by the type of device used and the setting in which one is employed, but reasonable generalizations can and should be made to focus preparedness. Graham Allison of Harvard University provides such an estimate to focus attention:

Even a crude device could create an explosive force of 10,000 to 20,000 tons of TNT, demolishing an area of about three square miles. Not only the World Trade Center, but all of Wall Street and the financial district and the lower tip of Manhattan up to Gramercy Park would have disappeared...In Washington, if such a vehicle (an SUV containing a nuclear device) exploded near the White House, an area reaching as far as the Jefferson Memorial would be immediately and completely destroyed, and a larger area, extending from the Pentagon to beyond the Capitol, would suffer damage equal to that caused to the Alfred P. Murrah Federal Building in Oklahoma City in 1995.[253]

Myth and Reality

Shortly after September 11, *Newsweek* reported that fallout from a "dirty bomb...could render an American city uninhabitable for years." In another report, environmentalist Harvey Wasserman pointed out that one or both of the planes that crashed into the World Trade Center could have instead crashed into two Hudson River atomic reactors at Indian Point.[254] He stated that such a crash would produce an "ensuing cloud of radiation... dwarf(ing) the ones at Hiroshima and Nagasaki," the result of which would be "...infants and small children (dying) quickly en masse...pregnant women spontaneously abort(ing) or giv(ing) birth to horribly deformed offspring...heart attacks, stroke and multiple organ failure (killing) thousands on the spot."[255]

The consequences described by Wasserman and *Newsweek* are contradicted in other analyses. Nuclear analysts argue a "change of years to days" for dirty bomb consequences; they have a short half-life.[256] Of nuclear reactor attacks Sharon Begley states:

It is physically impossible for the uranium used in U.S. power plants, which is typically less than five percent pure, to be fashioned into a Hiroshima-type bomb: nuclear bombs contain uranium that is closer to 90 percent pure. The real danger of a terror attack is the release of radioactive contaminants.

Expert contradictions confuse the public. Since abstraction is at the heart of complex systems, it is critical for information about them to be accurate, timely, and relevant among both experts and citizens. Weapons of mass destruction terrorism knowledge must be diffused throughout the nation. This need for information is traceable back to Three Mile Island, as indicated by civil defense expert, Tom Bethell:

We need to learn some basic facts about nuclear weapons. Yes, a blast would be horrific, and those who were too close would die immediately; nothing could save them. But we need to learning something about radiation. As the first crisis of its kind, all roads lead to Three Mile Island. Public fears of all things nuclear have been magnified by what can only be called a disinformation campaign, which has continued without interruption since the Three Mile Island accident of 1979.[257]

Learning more and blindly fearing less is exactly what will put disinformation to rest. Learning more about Three Mile Island is a good place to start.

Three Mile Island in a Nutshell: Six Chaotic Days from Wednesday, March 28 to Monday, April 2

No one died at Three Mile Island. No one was injured. The radiation release was negligible. The cost of the cleanup was just over a billion dollars, which is barely noticeable in national spending terms. The "only" long-term effects are psychological. Yet, Three Mile Island did happen, it never should have happened, and it was never anticipated. Once it occurred, it was permeated by a miasma of uncertainty as perception equaled reality. In sum, it was an accident and response mentality accentuated by the most uncertain of dynamics: the human condition.

Day One: Wednesday's Scramble[258]

At 4:00 am on March 28, 1979, a water pump in Three Mile Island's second nuclear reactor (i.e.: Three Mile Island - 2) stopped feeding water to its steam generators. No feedwater meant the reactor's coolant water began to heat up as the pressure inside the pressurizer tank above the reactor increased. As a result, the Pilot-Operated Relief Valve atop the pressurizer opened up to release the pressure. The release was not enough and the reactor "scrammed" eight seconds later. The control rods were dropped into the reactor's core to stop the nuclear fission process. Meanwhile, as the opened relief valve began to take effect, the reactor's core emergency cooling system automatically initiated its High Pressure Injection pumps, pumping over a thousand gallons of water a minute into the system to counteract the now falling pressure of the coolant system.

When this chain reaction began, the alarm board in the control room sounded. Due to faulty design, it would ring annoyingly and distractingly throughout the crisis. To cut it off meant an immediate loss of visible alarm indicator lights and later loss of any record of the crisis for posterity.[259]

There were more problems. After helping to drive the pressure of the system down by venting the steam and water, the relief valve did not close again. It was now an unguarded escape route for the coolant water. Operations center personnel did not recognize the loss of coolant signals. Their training dictated the system's only reliable coolant indicator was the water level in the pressurizer, which continued to rise as steam bubbles displaced the coolant water. Mistakenly interpreting steam for water, the operators were afraid that if the pressurizer filled with water (an event described as "going solid"), they would lose their ability to regulate the system's pressure. They thus concluded there was more than enough water in the coolant system and manually reduced the injection pumps to a rate of 100 gallons per minute, which could be offset by the still-opened relief valve.

The operators were unaware that two valves had been mistakenly closed for two days in violation of Nuclear Regulatory Commission (NRC) rules. In post-crisis reflection, one operator attributed this portion of the crisis to negligence, when he said, "It's easy to forget to open the valves. You can get distracted or you may be relieved in a change of shift."[260]

The problems that would ultimately form the crisis forever remembered as "Three Mile Island" were now in place: the combination of mechanical failure - a broken water pump and a stuck relief valve - and op-erator interference in the automatic safety system.

In less than two hours more than one-third of the reactor's coolant water escaped through the open relief valve. It was finally noticed and fixed at 6:22 am, but not before some radiation had been released into the atmosphere. If it had not been caught, the core would have been uncovered without its coolant long enough for a total meltdown, as concluded in one post-crisis study:

An eventual meltdown probably would have occurred, especially if one assumes that the operators cut off all water being pumped into the core...even with a core meltdown, there is only a small probability that the consequences of Three Mile Island would have been catastrophic to public health and safety...and the vast majority of the radioactive material released from the fuel would have been retained within the building.[261]

This potential for a meltdown - and more importantly, a meltdown's relatively benign consequences - was not known at the time, and good information like it would be hard to come by in the days ahead.

After declaring a site emergency, shift manager Bill Zewe alerted the following people and agencies that would comprise Three Mile Island's crisis management network:

- *The Plant Owner.* Walter Creitz, president of the plant's owner, Metropolitan Edison (Met Ed);
- *The Plant Owner's Parent Company.* Herman Dieckamp, president of Met Ed's parent company, General Public Utilities (GPU); Jack Herbein, GPU's vice president of generation;
- *The Emergency Managers.* The Pennsylvania Emergency Management Authority (PEMA);

PEMA followed its call from Zewe by notifying the Radiological Assistance Program of the Department of Energy; the Emergency Management Agency of Dauphin County (home of Harrisburg and Three Mile Island); the State Bureau of Radiation Protection (BRP); and the Governor's office;

• *The Federal Oversight Authority.* Region I office of the Nuclear Regulatory Commission (NRC). The NRC had been difficult to reach, because its phone directed to an answering machine until 8:00 am.[262] Once reached, three different voices were set in motion to speak for that organization during the crisis - one on site, one from a 70-specialist Incident Response Center in Bethesda, Maryland, and one from the five commissioners at Washington, D.C. NRC headquarters.

Noticeably missing from the contact list were local political authorities who would be most responsible for maintaining civil order. Harrisburg's mayor, Paul Doutrich, heard of the crisis through a surprising out-of-town radio station inquiry. Neighboring Middletown's mayor, Robert Reid, was not informed despite trying to call the plant for information. Reid's first day relates an important message:

All that I learned when I got to the office was that there had been an on-site emergency declared...so we sat there and we listened to the television...people were calling us who had relatives working down there and people just wanted to know what was going on. We couldn't give them any answers. We told them to call the county - we never did find out whether those people got through or not, the county's phones were so tied up.[263]

The public's introduction to the crisis was not smooth either. Around 8:00 am, "Captain Dave," a roving traffic reporter for Harrisburg's WKBO, picked up a Three Mile Island police transmission on his CB. After confirming a "general emergency" with plant owner Met Ed, WKBO aired it locally at 8:25 am.

The rest of the nation was first informed at 9:02 am, when the Associated Press ran a Three Mile Island line on its wire. The Pennsylvania public information officer followed the story by announcing the plant's "general emergency" status, but he could not define the status's meaning or relate specific emergency actions required of it. The plant's condition was clouded by use of a second term - "slight emergency" - but it too was not placed within a useful context for emergency managers or the public.[264]

The plant's official definition of a "general emergency" - its highest form of alert - was "an incident which has the potential for serious radiological consequences to the health and safety of the general public,"[265] but Three Mile Island personnel made no effort to mention this significance. The plant was struggling to get information to the public because its public relations staff could not interpret its technicians' technical memos that explained the incident. As a result, little day one information was passed to the public.[266]

Fulfilling his responsibility for the state's emergency preparedness, Lieutenant Governor William Scranton III held a press conference. He reported a small release of radiation but no danger to public health. His assurance was backed by the local radio news anchor who announced on the air that there was no danger.[267] These assurances contradicted the plant's emergency status and the facts. The public was almost immediately con-

founded when a Met Ed spokesman followed the press
conference by not confirming that radiation had been
released.

Interagency wrangling led to the formation of a
variety of uncoordinated crisis centers as experts tried
to understand why the reactor system was so hot. At the
plant itself, an emergency control team formed. Outside
of Philadelphia, the Nuclear Regulatory Commission's
(NRC's) Region I office activated its Incidence
Response Center and dispatched a five-member inspection team. The NRC and the Department of Energy
- interagency combatants in most every nuclear issue
- battled over which organization would monitor the
plant's radiation. As a result of the feud and a need to
justify a recently increased budget request, the far less
nuclear competent Environmental Protection Agency
split the bureaucratic difference and was put in charge
of the monitoring.[268] The Department of Energy had
already sent a mobile lab team from New Orleans; it
was sent home from as close as Altoona, Pennsylvania.
The Environmental Protection Agency team took two
days to assemble and arrive from Las Vegas.

The Virginia-based Three Mile Island plant designer,
Babcock & Wilcox, assembled and sent a response
team despite the fact it was not informed of the specific
problem. This team's value - its having worked an
almost identical relief valve crisis at Ohio's Davis
Besse reactor - was not understood. As a result, it too
was turned away - after arriving at the plant's doors.
The Three Mile Island operations center did not have
the wisdom to realize it was repeating the past.

Meanwhile, inside the plant, operators could not
start the reactor coolant pumps and continued to use the
one mechanism available to release heat - the original
broken relief valve - which now opened and closed

properly. Nothing seemed to work. Running out of possible solutions, a decision was made to depressurize the system so that flood tanks would automatically activate and cool the system. Although they did not know it, this action caused another loss of coolant and uncovered the core again.

After a 6-8 second hydrogen burn boomed with a large "thud," the two most experienced and senior officials present - plant station manager Gary Miller and Met Ed Vice President John Herbein - briefed Lieutenant Governor Scranton. Scranton was already upset with Herbein who, at an earlier Met Ed press conference, had decided not to tell reporters about the confirmation of radiation releases because the subject had not come up. Scranton later blasted Met Ed at an afternoon press conference, stating, "(the company) has given you and us conflicting information and has actually released radioactive steam without notifying the state." Scranton was wrong on this count, as steam had indeed been released, but it was not radioactive. It would not be the last conclusion based on a false premise that fanned the fires of misperception. Scranton's attack, though, was enough to impair Met Ed's credibility for the rest of the crisis.

After Herbein returned to the plant in the late afternoon, he authorized the repressuring of the reactor. The tactic worked and soon the coolant pumps were restarted. The plant returned to a relatively stable condition for the first time since 4:00 am that morning. Still, no one suspected any kind of meltdown.

At 5:00 pm the NRC issued a press release, which turned out to be day one's last mistake. Timed for the evening news, it suggested that the radiation readings outside the plant were not due to actual releases into the atmosphere; instead, they were the result of an absurd

possibility that radiation managed to penetrate the
four-foot wide steel-and-concrete walls of the reactor
containment building. The release was taken at face
value and had immediate impact. Walter Cronkite
ended his broadcast with the following Three Mile
Island report:

It was the first step in a nuclear nightmare...a
nuclear safety group said that radiation inside is...so
strong that after passing through a three-foot thick
concrete wall, it can be measured a mile away.

Tom Brokaw reported an NRC assessment that radiation has penetrated "through walls that were four
feet thick and it spread as far as ten to sixteen miles
from the plant." Instead of giving depth to a disaster,
the news media innocently played up a false statement
they had taken to be true.[269]

Day Two: Thursday's Calm before the Storm

NRC Chairman Hendrie began the day briefing on
Capitol Hill. On the heels of the recently released
movie, *The China Syndrome*, Congress questioned
Hendrie of a Three Mile Island meltdown. "Nowhere
near" was the response. Meanwhile, several con-
gressmen made the two-hour northwest trip to visit
the site, and the NRC sent a second team there. Also
noteworthy was an evacuation discussion among
Pennsylvania's health secretary, Gordon MacLeod,
emergency management director, Oran Henderson, and
the Director of the Bureau of Radiation Protection,
Thomas Gerusky. An evacuation would be limited
to pregnant women and young children, but both
Henderson and Gerusky recommended against one.

Thursday exposed the plant's lack of preparedness on an operational level. Lacking a full supply of respirators, plant personnel were prioritized based on their potential contributions; those who could be spared were sent home.[270] As many of the untested emergency procedures and much of the unused equipment proved to be, the respirators were unwieldy to use due to a combination of their bulky design and the operators' unfamiliarity with wearing them. As a result, plant managers "cheated" by repeatedly removing them while on the phone or performing other duties, thereby potentially exposing themselves to radiation in the process.[271]

Two evening events primed public perception and set the stage for Friday. First, with permission from the NRC, Met Ed alleviated its almost full water tanks by releasing 40,000 gallons of the slightly contaminated water into the Susquehanna River. Lieutenant Governor Scranton, thinking the state had not been informed, became again irritated with Met Ed. NRC Chairman Hendrie found out about the dumping only after it had started, ordered it stopped, and then had it resumed again once the state's Department of Environmental Resources accepted the near over-flowing tanks as justification.

Second, at Governor Thornburgh's press conference, the NRC's Charles Gallina informed the press that the danger had passed, the crisis was over. Gallina then returned to the plant to find data on the core that suggested damage much worse than previously considered. He called the Governor's office to pass the information and warn of the likelihood for further radiation release.

Later that night, Met Ed's parent company's [General Public Utilities (GPU)] engineers theorized the notion of a hydrogen bubble in the reactor. They based the theory on two unexplained events: the Wednesday

afternoon explosion and an increased collection of
non-condensables at the top of the reactor. A hydrogen
presence provided explanation for both. Hydrogen
did not condense, but it could be chemically explained
as the result of a core that must have melted in some
way. If the core had partially melted and created the
hydrogen bubble, the next question was whether or not
enough oxygen had entered the reactor to create a dangerously combustible condition. This possibility - later
proven to be unfounded - would dominate the crisis
until Monday.

Day Three: Friday - The Storm

By Friday morning, the reactor's means for removing
water - its "let-down system" - had deposited worrisome
levels of radioactive gases into the "make-up tank"
(a storage place for water to be added to the coolant
system). Normally, these gases would be compressed
and stored in the waste gas decay tanks. If any tanks
filled beyond capacity, an uncontrolled radiation release
could follow. Concerned about the make-up tank's
radioactive build-up, and aware that an unavoidable radioactive release would accompany transfer to the waste
gas decay tank, operations supervisor James Floyd considered a lesser of two evils and ordered radioactive
gas venting. He then requested a helicopter to take
radiation measurements, which came back with a report
of 1,200 millirems per hour, 130 feet above Three Mile
Island - 2 (i.e.: the second reactor).

Now concerned that the transferring vent would not
close properly, Floyd tried to alert PEMA but could
not get through. He then called Dauphin County's
emergency management office, told director Kevin
Molloy about the release, and asked Molloy to have

PEMA call him. PEMA returned the call and Floyd told PEMA to be prepared to evacuate the downwind civilian population. PEMA's director notified Lieutenant Governor Scranton. Scranton reported the information to Paul Critchlow in the Governor's office. Before reporting to the Governor, Critchlow checked the information with NRC liaison Karl Abraham, who called Washington.

In Washington, a senior NRC analyst was concerned about radiation releases from the almost full waste gas decay tanks. While briefing staff officials about his concern, Lake Barrett was asked what an off-site reading might be if the waste gas decay tanks released radiation. Barrett's calculation was 1,200 millirems per hour. No more than fifteen seconds after this deduction came Karl Abraham's call from Harrisburg reporting a 1,200 millirem per hour reading. Lost in translation was Barrett's analysis of potential off-site per hour radiation readings from a full waste gas decay tank's release.

The unlikely match of contextually irrelevant 1,200 millirem readings led to a misperceived notion that it was time to act. Harold Denton, the senior NRC official in the Barrett briefing, decided on a five-mile evacuation around Three Mile Island. Denton directed Harold Collins, the NRC Assistant Director for Emergency Preparedness, to notify Pennsylvania authorities. Collins called PEMA's Oran Henderson and made the recommendation. Based on entirely false data, the NRC officially recommended evacuation of an arbitrary radius around the stricken plant.

Upon receiving the recommendation, Henderson called Lieutenant Governor Scranton, who in turn told Governor Thornburgh. Henderson then called Dauphin County's Kevin Molloy, and thus completed the faulty decision cycle. Henderson told Molloy to expect an evacuation order in five minutes. Molloy promptly notified all fire departments within a ten mile radius of the plant as well as the local radio station, WHP, which broadcast an evacuation warning to the public.

Meanwhile the radiological protection office's Tom Gerusky (who had been notified by one of Henderson's aides), saw through the 1,200-millirem misperception because he knew about the original reading. Gerusky called the Governor to recommend against an evacuation but could not get through. At the plant the NRC's Charlie Gallina also saw the faulty logic and called Washington in hopes of getting a retraction of the evacuation.

Later reflecting on the misperception and its subsequent decision chain, NRC engineer Lake Barrett, said:

My perception was that we had shifted from a lack of information on things and nothing really firm to 'Well, here is a real piece of meaty information that has significance to it'. I believe it took a hypothetical situation and rather carved it in stone and set it on a mountain with a burning bush behind it...People immediately started talking about evacuation.

Evacuation momentum grew when warning sirens blared incessantly through Harrisburg streets and threw the unprepared community into unfortunate but predictable outcomes. People panicked. Private industry showed little restraint in making a buck off of the controversy. Car dealers made record profits selling automobiles to those seeking to leave town with reliable transportation, and the Camp Hill Cinema aired *The China Syndrome* and reinforced Hollywood's nuclear misperceptions to packed houses of movie-going citizens. A run on local bank reserves forced the Federal Reserve to send an additional $7 million cash to cover withdrawals.[272]

Over the sound of the sirens, Governor Thornburgh called NRC Chairman Joseph Hendrie who recommended against evacuation but suggested all five mile downwind citizens should stay inside. Thornburgh agreed. He also asked for the NRC to send a single point-of-contact to whom he could turn for reliable information. Thornburgh then went on WHP radio to calm the citizens.

Shortly after Thrornburgh's address, his press secretary, Paul Critchlow, briefed the press but mistakenly extended the potential evacuation zone to a ten mile radius, thereby increasing the affected population from 36,000 to 135,000. At this point the public was bombarded with simultaneous contradictions: officials stood before the press with public health assurances against an evacuation; reports on the size of a potential area of evacuation were conflicted; and local officials roamed the streets with bull horns ordering people to clear the streets, go home, and shut their windows.[273]

As the situation slid into chaos, President Carter called Governor Thornburgh. The White House would shape command of Three Mile Island into a system through which there would be one federal source of information, one press contact, one technical expert, one director for evacuation preparations, and a clear division of labor whereby the state would handle only emergency management and public safety information. The biggest change came in Carter's appointment of a single NRC representative, Harold Denton, with a communications package in support of him. Denton would also act as the link between the press, public, Governor's office, White House, and NRC.[274] Carter also appointed industry expert Jack Watson to do whatever was necessary on the nuclear end to resolve the crisis, and to use any portion of the rest of the industry as part of the solution to do so. One participant commented of Watson's task, "I think they need stem-to-stern reinforcements down here in many areas."[275]

Carter's move cut off information to several government agencies, and it was not strictly obeyed in line with its theoretical construct, but it did channel information through one source for the first time in the crisis. It also got the incident out of a bumbling, stumbling drama and into a focused crisis response that would ultimately lead to its closure.

With Carter's guidance in hand, the Governor called a meeting of key aides. The Secretary of Health's representative reminded the Governor of an idea to evacuate pregnant women and young children. Then Chairman Hendrie called to apologize for the NRC's 1,200 millirem mistake, after which Thornburgh asked Hendrie about an evacuation. Hendrie replied: "If my wife were pregnant and I had small children in the area, I would get them out because we don't know what is going to happen." The Governor made the following announcement:

Based on the advice of the chairman of the NRC, and in the interest of taking every precaution, I am advising those who may be particularly susceptible to the effects of radiation...pregnant women and pre-school age children...to leave the area within a five-mile radius of the Three Mile Island facility until further notice. We have also ordered the closing of any schools within this area. I repeat that this and other contingency measures are based on my belief that an excess of caution is best. Current readings are no higher than they were yesterday. However, the continued presence of radioactivity in the area and the possibility of further emissions lead me to exercise the utmost of caution.

That caution spread infectiously. The concern for pregnant women and children raised Three Mile Island's public health profile. In Washington, officials were worried that, if there was a serious radiation release, there would not be enough potassium iodide - a drug that prevented radioactive iodide from accumulating in the thyroid. They found no market for potassium iodide and no national stockpile of it.

Herman Dieckman, president of Met Ed's parent company, assembled a national Industry Advisory Group, whose first members would arrive on Saturday. Kevin Molloy, Dauphin County's emergency manager, had his five mile evacuation plan ready. But late Friday, PEMA directed preparations for a twenty mile radius evacuation of the six surrounding counties. The area now included 650,000 citizens, 13 hospitals, and a prison. Hospital evacuation had never before been considered, since there were none within a five mile radius and five miles is what Dauphin County had prepared for.

The announcement's psychological impact was acute. One pregnant woman recollected: "It was so frightening...I was crushed...I just thought, 'Oh, my God! This can't be happening. I can't believe it.'" Another woman recalled: "Everybody was running around. There was no order...I just picked up my kids and took them home and closed the windows and then just waited." A township official remembered: "Everything was in an uproar. It was very chaotic. We tried to come up with some kind of evacuation

system..." A local minister described the common fear
of the unknown:

> *Some people were tremendously depressed. Ladies*
> *were crying because they were separated from their*
> *husbands. Other people were so fighting mad that they*
> *would have gone and taken care of some people if they*
> *could have. Met Ed, the governor - they were mad at*
> *everybody.*[276]

Lacking information and not being prepared in any
way prior to the crisis, the public's anger was stimulated
by the xenophobia typical of the uniformed. Dr. Ernest
Sternglass, a professor of radiology at the University of
Pittsburgh, stirred panic in public broadcasts:

> *The reaction of the community should be to stand up*
> *and scream. I think they should protest violently about*
> *this whole matter of deciding not to warn the public,*
> *not to let the authorities know for many hours after this*
> *very serious situation developed.*[277]

Evacuation uncertainty reigned supreme. As the
local media fielded calls from the public and counseled
people to stay put, the media openly wondered whether
or not they themselves should leave.[278] Confusion
over an evacuation mounted when different areas
of government were calling for different actions;
the Secretary of Health called for an evacuation as
the Governor's office, plant, NRC, and PEMA were
counseling against it.[279] Caught in the awkward position
of arguing against while preparing for the evacuation,
PEMA personnel thought an evacuation would occur
for sure. According to Director Henderson, "from what

we had, and the way it was related to me, I was about ninety percent certain that we were going to execute an evacuation."

How the evacuation decision was made was not in line with standard incident command protocol. The decision was based on faulty information and ordered by the wrong individual for the wrong amount of people. There was no coordination with state or federal political authorities.[280] NRC investigator, Chuck Gallina said:

I was mad. They were circumventing the licensee's procedures and circumventing the state's procedures... they notify the Bureau of Radiological Protection, so you have two intelligent people who at least know the jargon and meaning of the stuff, and if they agree, then the site or the state may make a recommendation and they go to the governor for the order...but it was done directly from the NRC headquarters, which has no business recommending evacuation of anyone, and it had gone to Civil Defense, which doesn't know what these numbers mean, and it caused a panic.[281]

The old confusion on how far to evacuate cropped up again. Civil defense directors had been planning for a five-mile evacuation for two days in line with Pennsylvania's emergency plan. The NRC arbitrarily declared a ten-mile evacuation, which caused confusion because 5-10 mile staging points were ready for the five-mile evacuation. Local civil defense directors began to activate public safety personnel, and one county director warned the public to get ready. He waited for a call from the governor to execute the evacuation, and the call never came.[282]

In the meantime, Met Ed's Jack Herbein had another

tough time with the press. During his Friday press
conference, before which he had known nothing of
the 1,200-millirem reading, he sealed his irrelevance
for the duration of the crisis. Totally frustrated at one
point, Hebrein responded: "I don't know why we
need to...tell you each and everything that we do specifically." Herbein's complete inadequacy with the
press, combined with White House concerns of conflicting reports going to the press, solidified Carter and
Thornburgh's earlier decision to use Harold Denton as
the single voice for the duration of the crisis.

The NRC held a Washington press conference at
which it acknowledged what was theoretically obvious:
a meltdown, while remote, was possible. With the
first official link between the accident and *The China
Syndrome*, United Press International (UPI) broke the
story by early evening: "Three Mile Island Accident
Poses the Ultimate Risk of Meltdown."

The plant's experts were now fully aware that they
had a hydrogen bubble on their hands. Harold Denton
was informed that the bubble was 1,000 cubic feet. It
could push the coolant below the core, uncovering it
once again. The second issue, whether or not such
a bubble could create an explosion similar to the
hydrogen burn on Wednesday morning, still hinged
on whether or not oxygen had accessed the reactor
chamber. Although NRC Chairman Hendrie told
Governor Thornburgh there was no chance, he was
increasingly preoccupied with the possibility. Hendrie
asked the NRC staff for a new explosion probability
analysis. As the bubble consumed plant operations, the
White House closed the day with a press conference,
at which Press Secretary Jody Powell downplayed the
meltdown potential as "speculative."

Day Four: Saturday's Misinformation

Saturday started with positive news - health officials located a producer of potassium iodide. St. Louis-based Mallinckrodt Chemical Company agreed to work around the clock in order to produce 230,000 one-ounce bottles of the drug (The delivery was eventually made in increments beginning four days and ending eight days after the crisis began between Sunday, April 1 and Wednesday, April 4).

Although it arrived too late for maximum effectiveness, the drug news was viewed as a victory at the time. But, even that good news was subsumed by the double-edged exposure/explosion potential of the hydrogen bubble. Shut out from Three Mile Island since day one, plant designer Babcock & Wilcox worked off-site to produce relevant analysis but could not get an audience with decision making authorities. The analysis asserted there was no excess oxygen in the reactor that could combustibly combine with hydrogen generated from the damaged core. Chairman Hendrie later admitted his fears of a reactor explosion were groundless, but on this Saturday he was the NRC's only bona fide reactor expert, and, unfortunately, the only opinion that really mattered. If he was concerned about an explosion, then by default so was the country. At an afternoon press conference, Hendrie told the nation that a "flammable mixture" might result at Three Mile Island.

Met Ed's John Herbein held his last press conference before announcing that Harold Denton would speak for the plant's status. He informed the press of the hydrogen bubble's one-third reduction since Friday and indicated the crisis was over. Ironically, Herbein was right, but at this point, he had no credibility. Denton denied Herbein's analysis and thus fanned the fires of press and public confusion. Following the denial, Associated Press (AP) reporter Stan Benjamin submitted a story that warned of the bubble's imminent explosion within as little as two days. Checked line-by-line with the NRC's public information and chairman's staff, the story's accuracy was confirmed before it ran on the wire.

After reading the story, Governor Thornburgh angrily ordered his press secretary, Paul Critchlow, to call Harold Denton. Denton came to the statehouse and held an 11:00 pm press conference with Governor Thornburgh. Refuting the analysis, the Governor stated:

There is no imminent catastrophic event fore-seeable at the Three Mile Island facility...I appeal to all Pennsylvanians to display an appropriate degree of calm and resolve and patience in dealing with this situation.

Damage control failed. The public did not know who or what to believe. Those directly responsible for an evacuation were in the worst position, caught as they were between dueling analyses, the need to maintain order, and the need to execute an orderly evaluation. In Washington, the Department of Health continued to debate the size of the evacuation. Their discussions were academic as the NRC never made any attempt to seek public health advice.

The AP story exemplified the press's inability to tell the Three Mile Island story short of pure fiction. One science writer said of the AP what could have applied to every major source of press communications coming out of the crisis: "Don't accept any wire stuff out of Harrisburg. The AP (doesn't) know what it (is) doing."[283] Journalists did not understand the complex technical issues being discussed; they were assigned to a story that began overnight and unfolded very quickly. Their value was proximity, not expertise.

Day Five: Sunday's Emergence from the Storm

The Department of Health was not the only agency cut out of the decision making loop. Since it had over-reacted to the possibility of an evacuation on Friday, PEMA had not been invited to the state executive meetings. Although clearly understandable given the scare they had created, PEMA and local officials were still necessary if an evacuation had to be implemented. Local community officials were also growing uneasy about state and federal coordination. Things were so bad in Dauphin County that a state senator called Lieutenant Governor Scranton very early Sunday morning and threatened him with a 9:00 am Dauphin County evacuation if cooperation did not improve.

President Carter paid a Sunday visit to the plant - a bold move given the remaining uncertainties. As with most Presidential visits, it was mostly symbolic, but symbolism mattered in an otherwise invisible crisis. Residents intuitively recognized that if it was safe enough for the President of the United States to be there, it was safe enough for them.

Meanwhile, the NRC was still hot on the explosion theory and continued to warn of a possible evacuation. But by the end of the day, Chairman Hendrie's advisors convinced him that an explosion was highly unlikely. Reversing its position after having started and fanned the bubble story, the NRC never issued a public re-traction.

Day Six: Monday's Closure to the Immediate Response

At a morning press conference, Harold Denton revealed that the bubble had been dramatically reduced.
The crisis was essentially over. A week later Governor
Thornburgh rescinded his five mile advisory for
pregnant women and pre-school children. On April 27,
Three Mile Island - 2 was placed in a "natural circulation" cooling mode.

Teachable Moments of Three Mile Island

History should never repeat as "another Three Mile
Island." The nuclear industry's risk management and
oversight have been forever changed. Should Leningrad
or any of the world's other nuclear power plants experience a similar tragedy that central Pennsylvania
narrowly avoided, they will do so with clear knowledge
of the technical and managerial issues that led to the
consequences. Now, Three Mile Island's insights must
also be applied against the challenges of weapons of
mass destruction terrorism and other complex systems.

"It Could Never Happen"

Preparedness comes from ordinary people behaving
according to social norms and expectations. At Three
Mile Island those norms and expectations were based
on false premises - from the plant's design, to its operations, to its crisis management, to its community
preparedness, to its oversight and regulatory support.
The mythology that permeated throughout the nuclear
industry prior to Three Mile Island was accurately
captured by both the fictitious operations center protagonist in *The China Syndrome* and a Three Mile

Island reporter. The actor held an unbending belief of his nuclear power plant, thinking, "every single thing that could possibly go wrong has been considered."[284] The reporter wrote of industry fantasy in real terms:

Optimistic thinking...pervad(ed) the nuclear industry. So small were the chances of a major accident and so fail-safe the emergency systems, that certain accidents and situations didn't even have to be considered in emergency planning...The industry was so confident that a bad accident would not take place that it felt little need to make emergency plans in case one did.[285]

The industry's fail-safe mentality lulled the public to sleep, as exemplified in a Met Ed letter to Three Mile Island's surrounding citizens:

Even the worst possible accident postulated by the Atomic Energy Commission would not require an evacuation of the borough of Middletown...it can be seen that it is unnecessary to have specific evacuation routes...[286]

Appeased by such gestures, most citizens did not want to know the consequences of merely living in their zip code. As one local woman said, "I always hated to think what might happen...so I didn't."[287]

When the public did get interested, which was only with the crisis upon it, it was too late. And, once interested, they sought the wrong source for accurate information: Hollywood. "This is not *The China Syndrome!*" had to be reinforced over and over again to an unknowledgeable public. One citizen articulated what many believed: "You take the combination of the

movie and the event, and it brings it right down to your
doorstep. Like they say, the plant could blow straight to
China."[288]

Three Mile Island's first general lesson for weapons
of mass destruction and other complex systems is:
threats are real; they happen. It is only human to
ignore horrific events as inconceivable or believe them
to be beyond one's control. But, such folly does not
make them any less likely to occur. Bioterror expert
Richard Preston warns the general public to confront
hard science, shed its fictions, and understand its
reality: "We can help exorcise our demons a little bit by
knowing more about them."[289]

"What is Important?"

Public health is the sina qua non of the modern crisis.
In the system that comprised Three Mile Island, public
health was not central to an industry, a company, or the
public. An industry sought to establish itself as the
country's premier source of energy, a company sought
ever-higher returns on investment and the opportunity
to build more plants, and the public was served with a
ridiculously inexpensive source of power. The crisis
took its shape accordingly - the NRC, politicians, and
plant operators were in charge. In contrast, public
health and emergency management officials (who
were responsible for moving the public to safety in an
evacuation) were an afterthought in this crisis; at times,
they were no thought at all.

Three Mile Island's crisis formed years before
1979, its culture hardened by a central economic
focus. Economy drove three major systemic issues:
massive mandatory overtime, safety shortfalls, and
worker dissatisfaction.[290] In this respect a plant merely

reflected its industry; nuclear power held a long standing reputation of sacrificing safety and working conditions in favor of delivering cheap, profitable energy. One Three Mile Island manager said, "There are no regulations limiting the number of hours per day or year workers can be on the job in the nuclear power industry."[291] One worker commented, "I've seen guys work around the clock, 24 or 32 hours...you just go, go, go...It's crazy."[292] Another quit the plant, claiming, "I was dissatisfied with management and safety precautions and shortcuts."[293]

The fact that construction costs for Three Mile Island - 2 ran well over projections only exacerbated the economic pinch by forcing a series of ugly business-first decisions. Workers characterized it as "a rush job," stating, "they were on you all the time...saying let's get it done; we got to get back up there; we got to get on-line."[294]

Economy spilled over into the plant's inability to manage the crisis without seriously endangering the public. One of Governor Thornburgh's staffers summed up what he believed was plant owner Met Ed's approach at the outset: "I knew that their M.O. was likely to be minimal...to minimize all these kinds of events...from that moment on, we virtually had nothing to do with Met Ed."[295]

Three Mile Island shocked an unknowing government and citizenry that had enjoyed nuclear power's economic benefits and the presence of a big regional employer. They had also accepted the industry's line on safety. In the case of Three Mile Island, ignorance was not bliss.

Citizens must be prepared for crises before they occur, the mental preparation as important as the physical response and recovery. "Collective identity" is a concept that explains how and why communities prepare and mobilize.[296] Communities share group definitions, interests, and experiences that form solidarity and emotions, which lead to civic activism. Three Mile Island's collective identity was far from one of determined action. Instead of grassroots organizations forming to prepare for and respond to a disaster in the community, Three Mile Island's collective plant, community, safety, and crisis response identity was one of inaction and inattention. Even a typical "us versus them" grassroots movement mentality was missing because all parties felt a part of the disinterested "us."

Following the crisis, the community still failed to form the tight bonds required of a response, thereby exacerbating public health effects of a situation that ironically had few direct physical consequences. Immediately after Three Mile Island stabilized, a county mental health officer noted, "When this dies down, I think it will hit us. A lot of people will want to talk about what they went through, that they felt inadequate in the crisis and embarrassment at being scared."[297]

When it did die down, though, the collective identity never shifted to one of information sharing and action from one of ignorance and isolation, as observed by a local physician: "The people are not addressing the (psychological) problem...it's like a powder keg waiting to explode."[298] A symptom of flagging community health, Three Mile Island area mothers experienced "acute and chronic mental health effects," with more than half in a major study wrongly perceiving the situation as still dangerous nine months later.[299]

The public health lesson was never learned in Three Mile Island, and it has not taken hold beyond it for primary consideration in weapons of mass destruction preparedness. Today's communities are no better prepared than those that surrounded Three Mile Island. Their professional public health support system is no better off either, as indicated by co-chairs of the U.S. Commission on National Security, Gary Hart and Warren Rudman:

Many local public health departments are barely funded...medical professionals often lack the training to properly diagnose and treat diseases spawned by biological agents. Many of the states' public health reporting systems are antiquated, slow, and outmoded.[300]

Uncertainty Reigns

Of Three Mile Island's decision making, the Presidentially-sanctioned Kemeny Commission concluded:

The response to the emergency was dominated by an atmosphere of almost total confusion. There was a lack of communication at all levels. Many key recommendations were made by individuals who were not in possession of accurate information, and those who managed the accident were slow to realize the significance and implications of the events that had taken place.[301]

That there was a shortage of information from which to make decisions is not surprising. Facts are scare when complex systems go awry. That communications were absent at all levels, and that decisions were made by individuals who could not grasp the implications of their decisions, is unacceptable. Three Mile Island's decision making ineptness stands out at all levels, it most clearly evidenced three days into the crisis when no one still knew what was going on or had a workable process to find out. The senior federal nuclear expert, NRC Chairman Joseph Hendrie, admitted, "we are operating almost totally in the blind. (Governor Thornburgh's) information is ambiguous, mine non-existent...I don't know, it's like a couple of blind men staggering around making decisions."[302]

Without a way to get reliable information, the public predictably panicked, and asked what to do: "Is it true that once I leave my house I won't be able to come back for a hundred years?" "What should I do with my dog?" "If I leave now, will I be able to come back next Tuesday?"[303] Their answers came from people who did not know and had nowhere to turn to find out.

The lesson of *uncertainty* is to *expect* misinformation and a shortage of facts - *expect the unexpected* - regardless of how ill or well prepared a response may be. Decision makers must be prepared to make decisions with a lack of concrete information; they will rely on precisely what was missing at Three Mile Island and must be built for weapons of mass destruction preparedness: experience, wisdom, knowledge, and training. They must also develop and then rely on a preconceived crisis management framework that Three Mile Island also lacked. Such a framework will produce the best possible information from uncertainty and communicate decisions throughout the network and to the public as a crisis unfolds.

Reducing Uncertainty: A Group of Experts

Three Mile Island's uncertainty flowed not just from a lack of information and misinformation but also from a paucity of individuals who truly understood the dynamics of a nuclear crisis. Author Peter Stillman's account summarizes the shortfall:

The nuclear power plant itself was not understood sufficiently well for individuals to recognize the significance and implications of the information they had.[304]

This effect is undeniable and points to the need for a group of "experts." The so-called "experts" at Three Mile Island did more than anyone could have imagined to exacerbate the problem. In effect, they were not "expert" - they were not prepared, did not know what to do, and could not learn from the past. The only bright spot was the ability of the private sector to organize its expertise and deploy it to the scene of the accident. A hastily arranged Industry Advisory/Three Mile Island Recovery Group eventually included over 800 experts. Their sustained purpose was to maintain the plant in a safe condition, contain the release of radioactivity, and make a reliable and safe transition.[305]

The post-Three Mile Island nuclear industry has established a team of experts who possess collective wisdom through a wide range of functional expertise, general knowledge of many different nuclear crises, and the capability to move on a moment's notice to address a crisis as soon as one unfolds. The Department of Energy's Nuclear Emergency Support Team (NEST) maintains a 1,000-member, task-organized nuclear "national guard" of leading physicists, engineers, conventional explosives experts, and chemists, among others.[306] This package includes many features needed but missed at Three Mile Island: four types of physicists (i.e.: nuclear, infrared, atmospheric, and health); engineers; chemists; mathematicians; and communications, logistics, management, and public information personnel.[307]

The weapons of mass destruction terrorism response community should incorporate a NEST-like capability among its many independent and isolated (nuclear and non-nuclear terrorism) rapid reaction law enforcement, military, emergency management, fire, and public health services. Recommendations have been made by experts to dramatically increase National Guard weapons of mass destruction civil support teams, enhance state and local expertise, and tap private sector expertise.[308] The garnering of expertise is important - and one-half of the battle. Integrating that expertise from a disjointed collection of independent rapid reaction capabilities into a coordinated response is just as vital.

Political Leadership

While coordinated expertise will reduce uncertainties that come from both a lack of information and an inability to interpret the information, there is no substitute for leadership. For example, President Carter was clearly engaged in Three Mile Island, yet he did not micro-manage the effort. His office supported Pennsylvania with everything that it needed. Most importantly, Carter established one voice for the crisis by providing his personal representative, the thinking behind this brilliant stroke revealed to his press secretary, Jody Powell:

There are too many people talking. And my impression is that half of them don't know what they are talking about...Get those people to speak with one voice.[309]

The other Three Mile Island leader, Governor Thornburgh, had an intuitive sense for the unprecedented nature of this event. Regarding the potential evacuation, Thornburgh told the President's Commission on Three Mile Island:

This type of evacuation had never been carried out before on the face of this earth, and it is an evacuation that was quite different in kind and quality than one undertaken in time of flood or hurricane or tornado... When you talk about evacuating people within a 5-mile radius of the site of a nuclear reactor, you must recognize that that will have 10-mile consequences, 20-mile consequences, 100-mile consequences...This is to say, it is an event that people are not able to see, to hear, to taste, to smell.[310]

With such understanding, Thornburgh was very careful about how and when he spoke directly to the public. When the time came to issue an evacuation order, he specifically avoided use of the word itself. When the AP story broke about an impending hydrogen explosion, Thornburgh immediately summoned the single point of contact (i.e.: Harold Denton) and held an 11 pm press conference. Whenever possible, the Governor led Three Mile Island from the front.

Both the President and the Governor did not rush to speak without the facts as they best knew them. Given the difficult circumstances, they calmly sought out the best information possible. Nowhere in the Three Mile Island record is there even a hint of criticism regarding their personal involvement; both leaders are distinguished by their relative absence from the crisis's numerous critiques.

Communications

Communications of information to and from the public is another issue on which Three Mile Island sheds light. For information exchange, there is no substitute for a good spokesperson, which presents Three

Mile Island's paradoxical example of Harold Denton. Denton was the man the public most trusted, especially after Met Ed's series of misleading statements. A third party report summarized Denton as:

A man of easy confidence and a nonabrasive manner, Denton (projects) an image of a person who, if he does not have the answers, will be willing to look for them and to share them once they are found.[311]

Another said:

Denton's calm demeanor and constant optimism were as reassuring as his frankness was refreshing, and the White Knight won instant credibility. In their eagerness to invest him with authority, reporters called him Doctor Denton, although he has only a bachelor of science degree from North Carolina State.[312]

Denton was not perfect, but in a crisis, perfection is not the standard of measurement - competence is. Denton had overreacted to the 1,200 millirem reading and recommended a central Pennsylvania evacuation from his Washington, D.C. office. He also refused to deny the explosive danger of the hydrogen bubble for two days after it had been reduced, which kept the emergency psychology unnecessarily alive. In the end though, when he was ordered by President Carter to speak as the one voice for the crisis, he was the one trusted by the press and public and there can be no mistaking the assuaging effect that he had on them.

Denton's success was critical, because the press is a central player in crisis communications, and it had a poor track record with pre-Three Mile Island nuclear issues. Nuclear stories provided no image for television, no clear description for radio, and difficult terms and context for print. Lacking the broad appeal of other issues and complicated by the scientific nature, reporters shied away from the nuclear industry. The industry perpetuated the ignorance by putting off the press during nuclear accidents, and downplaying issues as quickly as they surfaced.[313] This symbiotically distant relationship was followed by Three Mile Island and its reporters who "dumped Met Ed weekly releases right into the circular file - unopened."[314]

Although both the press and the industry needed an advanced and understanding relationship to provide enlightened communications to the public, it could not be created during the crisis. For the uninformed press, Three Mile Island finally provided something newsworthy - the perfect accident at the perfect place at the perfect time. The *China Syndrome* had just hit the big screen purporting meltdown consequences as far as an "area the size of Pennsylvania." Harrisburg was just two hours from the country's two big press hubs: Washington and New York. Aside from not knowing science, Three Mile Island reporters did not do even basic research and were therefore incapable of providing the in-depth coverage that was their alleged mantle. One study of reporters and editors, for example, found that none knew that Three Mile Island - 2 had been shut down for two-thirds of its trial days before officially opening in 1978.[315]

An unprepared media preparation was forced to blindly rely on technical expertise. Sources had to be accepted at face value. There were no stories, for example, on whether those involved in Three Mile Island crisis management really knew how to deal with its problems. As the NRC's Roger Mattson reflected on the AP hydrogen bubble account: "The explosion story may have been blown out of proportion by the press, but it originated with our staff."[316]

Another symptom of an uninformed media was that it did not differentiate coverage of fear from their coverage of analysis. This problem was captured by reporters Peter Sandman's and Mary Padman's post-crisis account:

Newspapers and networks regularly crossed the line between covering people's fears (legitimate and important) and letting those fears represent the actual situation (misleading and unfair). The words of a dairy farmer who claims he's afraid to drink his own animals' milk more than balance official statements that the milk is safe - especially when the farmer is positioned to speak for both sides.[317]

The Three Mile Island lesson for reporters was provided by Charles Shaw of Lancaster, Pennsylvania's *Intelligencer-Journal*:

You have to really understand what people are saying - you must really know it. Otherwise you get half-truths all the time and you miss the guts of the issue.[318]

Government also learned a press communications lesson. Until the single point of contact was established, every government agency - at all levels - handled the press and public differently. And, none did it particularly well. As one example, the NRC filtered and batch-processed its questions and answers. The process was so cumbersome that reporters went elsewhere for information. As a second example, Pennsylvania's gubernatorial human/politico design produced a new governor with a strong, trusted press secretary. The press secretary handled the crisis at the staff level as a de facto chief of staff, the result of which severely bottlenecked information to the press and public. Lacking a press secretary with whom to communicate, the press felt alienated.

Training Versus Education

Governor Thornburgh scraped the tip of the iceberg when he asked Three Mile Island's big takeaway question: "Is there anyone in the country who has experience with the health consequences of such a release?"[319] The answer was "yes and no." Yes, there were people who had experience with such a release. No, they could not apply that experience as information at the plant. No, the operators inside the plant were not properly educated to respond to something that was not in the operations manual. No, much of the industry as a whole was not educated in such a way either.

The pre-Three Mile Island nuclear industry was comprised of trained, "by the book" technicians. While training is important, the industry was not educated, intuitively knowledgeable, and wise enough to react to issues that fell outside of a textbook solution. Operators followed emergency procedures - procedures that did not require them to think; they were just supposed to react. They were required to pass examinations based on emergency procedures; they were not educated in the deeper issues of engineering or physics; and they needed no more than a high school degree as terms of employment. According to Three Mile Island chronicler, Mark Stephens, "beyond the emergency procedures and the reactor, operators are lost." [320] This fact was made clear on day one when operators followed procedure and held back high-pressure injection water (while allowing the system to drain) even though their suspicions were to ignore the operations center readings and force-feed the water.[321] *The China Syndrome* acted out the education disparity when its trained technical analyst said, "The book says you can't do it!" and its educated operations center manager responded, "Screw the book!"[322]

Beyond the plant were even starker education and training deficiencies. Among emergency managers, there were no formal training requirements for civil defense directors at state or local levels. The Commonwealth of Pennsylvania required the posting of civil defense positions, but the individuals who qualified to staff the posts needed no particular competencies, attended no mandatory training, and were not required to have any formal education.[323]

The education lesson applies beyond Three Mile Island. First, as crises mount in their technical and scientific complexity, the number of United States scientists in many critical academic disciplines is declining. "We risk losing a critical mass of knowledge," says the University of Missouri's reactor program director. Enrollments in nuclear science programs declined between 3-15% annually from 1980-1992.[324] These classes fill the middle and upper management ranks of nuclear power today.

Second, the weapons of mass destruction terrorism response community is neither trained nor educated. From 1996-1999 the federal government provided basic response training to only 134,000 of the nation's 9 million first responders.[325] State and local homeland security "experts" have no common standards or requisite expertise, their varying knowledge and background ranges from law enforcement to retired military to National Guard to public health depending on the state or locality. Today's first responders lack a major post-Three Mile Island recommendation of "sufficient diagnostic ability to deduce and respond to events that may not be the same as those prescribed in the training programs."[326]

The public also needs to be appropriately trained and educated about the crises it faces. A contemporary educational strategy that bridges scientists and communities through public participation is conducted through the Danish Board of Technology. The Danish convene "consensus conference" lay panels whose citizen-members are trained in complex systems. According to the *American Journal of Public Health*, more than 20 such panels have been held on subjects such as genetically modified foods, the human genome project, and air pollution.[327]

Systems Design

If a complex system is poorly designed, no amount of human effort in preparations, operations, or response will alleviate a disaster. Design issues go beyond the physical to include the bureaucratic. In both traditional nuclear and weapons of mass destruction preparedness, design is significantly influenced by interplay among industry, community, and government.

Three Mile Island's design problems give notice to other systems, for they began before the plant was even built. The nuclear industry's approval process was long and unwieldy; consequently, it was easier to adapt a less than perfect existing facilities model from another General Public Utilities (i.e.: Met Ed's parent company) plant than to go through a cumbersome approval process for a new model tailored to central Pennsylvania's needs.

Three Mile Island was also poorly system-designed - it required a lot of interaction among its disparate parts. Three Mile Island touted a strategy outlined in *The China System* - the "defense in depth" - whereby there are "backup systems of backup systems of backup systems."[328] Unfortunately, the strategy fails when elements that tie a system together are not truly redundant but are actually dependant on one another. A single failure or malfunction in any number of areas had the dual potential to both cause an accident and disable protective measures to prevent the very same accident. The relief valve situation exemplifies the problem. An Atomic Energy Commission study estimated the chance of relief valve failure to be 1 million to 1; it never factored in Three Mile Island's cause - deliberate human error - in the odds for valve closure.[329]

A Process of Preparedness: Mitigation, Planning, Response, and Recovery

Mitigation

As with all of the preparedness steps, Three Mile Island fell short in mitigation. Two events showcase the shortfall. First, on the morning of day one, retired engineer Bill Whittock tasted a strange metallic substance in the air. When he looked up a telephone number to alert the state civil defense office, he could not find it - the agency's name had changed to the Pennsylvania Emergency Management Agency.[330] Whittock may not have been able to provide any new or relevant information to lesson the effects of the crisis, but he should have been in a position to do so. Whittock is just one bit player among many whose ability to provide or receive information or otherwise lessen Three Mile Island's severity was blocked. As Three Mile Island did, most complex crises form not from one big problem but through the interplay of many small problems at a particular point in time.

A second example is available in the Governor's office, where mitigation should have been job one. An unprepared state government did not think to run through the steps that could have lessened the effects of a radiological disaster once one occurred. On evacuation day Governor Thornburgh revealed the lack of mitigation consideration prior to the crisis as illustrated by a press question:

Governor, there are, as you know, a series of recommendations that the state has the power to make. I think the most simple among them is just that area residents close their windows. Have any of those recommendations been suggested so far?[331]

The answer was no.

The state also failed its pubic health mitigation role. First, there was no psychological preparation. Residents did not seek out assistance from mental health facilities, and mental health training was not provided for pubic officials, physicians, clergy, and other visible community leaders to recognize and allay the public's anxiety and depression.[332] Second, there was no counter-radiation treatment among Three Mile Island's communities. Identified as a protective agent in a well circulated pre-Three Mile Island report by the National Council on Radiation Protection and Measurement, potassium iodide still had no drug companies producing it. Its short shelf-life and lack of commercial uses limited producer interest. Pennsylvania did not find the drug important enough to stockpile. When crisis priorities are set, and public health mitigation is the sina qua non, innovative solutions emerge. In England, for example, potassium iodide is stored in electric meter boxes around nuclear power plants.[333] Meter readers exchange the old stock for new in the course of their monthly rounds.

Planning

Planning is a comprehensive, ongoing process that involves all crisis constituencies and also clearly defines the lines of authority and communications necessary to make preparatory, response, and recovery decisions. If conducted properly, planning is estimated to reduce casualties in weapons of mass destruction crises by as much as 60% in some scenarios.[334] Contemporary public health crisis planning, an area in which Three Mile Island fell considerably short, is characterized by experts David Kriebel and Joel Tickner:

Broader public participation processes may in-crease the quality, legitimacy, and accountability of complex decisions...more effective processes for in-volving affected communities could increase trust in government. Such processes must be both fair and competent, meaning that they allow all those who want to participate to have substantive access to the decision-making process from the beginning and that they provide financial and technical resources so citizens can participate on equal terms with experts. In addition, there must be clearly defined mechanisms by which citizen input is fed into the policymaking process.[335]

Planning at Three Mile Island was not inclusive. It was conducted only by experts, and it was not complete. Plans were not shared outside of the specific organization or functional discipline in which they emerged. Unfortunately, this same conundrum continues to define many complex systems today, to include weapons of mass destruction preparation. Some specific Three Mile Island shortfalls that could provide planning foresight are described below:

- *The Drug Shortage.* As previously mentioned, when Three Mile Island was upon the nation, there was no knowledge of where or how to supply citizens with potassium iodide in the event of a disaster. When September 11 again joined the nation in a commonly shared trauma, it still lacked significant stores of that drug (and many others necessary to lessen the effects of other dangerous chemical, radiological, or biological agents). It was only after September 11 that the Department of Health and Human Services bought 1.6 million doses and planned to purchase another 6 million doses.[336]
- *Crisis Communications Plans.* The plant's communications plan left out many necessary participants, to include the local political authorities. The NRC's regional office protocols lacked even the basic ability to monitor the phones in place of an answering machine until 8 am. None of the crisis's organizational participants at local, state, or federal levels had planned for secure phone or courier communications. As a result, phones were busy, key information was not exchanged, and sub-optimal decisions were made throughout the six days by people who were available to make them, even if those people were not in the best experiential or authoritative positions to do so.

• *Decision Making and Decision Authority Structure.*
The decision making process was unclear because
participants had not planned and trained in it. As
a result, decisions were made by offices, agencies,
or individuals without the authority to make them.
Those in positions of authority then openly wondered
how the crisis was unraveling out of their control.
Three Mile Island's governing (i.e.: federal, state,
and local) and functional (i.e.: on-site, technical,
nuclear, emergency management, and public health)
lines of authority were not clearly understood by
crisis participants. Even within specific government
agencies, decision making was not agreeable, which
led to (and will always to lead to) disruptive decisions being made in the heat of the moment. Years
after Three Mile Island, the NRC still could not
agree where its decision making authorities should
be stationed in order to avoid Three Mile Island's
factionalization of opinion and information.[337]

• *State Planning.* The Commonwealth of Pennsylvania
had emergency plans, but they were overly optimistic,
conducted internally, and not widely known in
interagency or public circles. PEMA, in particular,
was driven by an insular military mindset, yet
military efficiency will never define an urban civilian
evacuation. Its evacuation plans assumed 8.5 million
people could be moved from strategic parts of
Pennsylvania within 32 hours, while the Harrisburg
Police estimated 20 hours to evacuate the capital
alone.[338] During the evacuation itself is not a time to
learn (or disabuse another organization) of unrealistic
logistical assumptions.

• *Local Planning.* No community within five miles
of the plant had a formal, published evacuation
plan.[339] According to the Kemeny Commission:

We found an almost total lack of detailed plans in the local communities around Three Mile Island. It is one of the many ironies of this event that the most relevant planning by local authorities took place during the accident. In an accident in which prompt defensive steps are necessary within a matter of hours, insufficient advance planning could prove extremely dangerous.[340]

Plans did not exist because of a lack of interest. The public simply believed Met Ed when it said that no evacuation plans were needed because no danger existed. Although some local county emergency planners disagreed, they could not muster other local officials and volunteers to create a plan.[341] As a result, the public had no knowledge of how to perform many basic response actions, such as conduct an orderly evacuation of their homes and communities. Shifting to present day, many areas vulnerable to attack have the same lack of community planning - even after September 11 - that Three Mile Island's communities did. As of 2002, for example, Washington, D.C. - the most likely metropolitan weapons of mass destruction target in the United States - had no biological or radiological detection plans.[342]

• *On-Site Planning.* The plant itself maintained some semblance of planning but clearly not enough. For example, its wastewater tanks almost filled during the crisis, but no one expected an accident to last more than a day. No one thought tanks would ever fill.[343] On an even more embarrassing level, the plant's quality control officer was not listed in the crisis plans and was therefore locked out during the crisis. A failure to control quality is precisely what caused Three Mile Island.

• *Third Party Planning.* Corporations, non-profit organizations, hospitals, and other established entities must also figure crisis planning into their daily routines. As one observer noted after the fact for such organizations, "reasonable emergency action plans should include a set of pre-established responses, graded according to the probability of the risk, as well as to the severity of the effects that might be incurred."[344] Using this standard, the best evacuation plan belonged to ABC News. Based on its standard on-site emergency planning, ABC compiled a logical six-page plan with two contingency fallback positions outside of a twenty-mile radius.[345]

• *Press Contingency Planning.* The press had no plans for this type of crisis. Its science writers were not on-call to respond to a nuclear contingency. As a result, uninformed political reporters were dispatched to cover an issue they could not comprehend. The lack of comprehension led to reports of inaccurate information and the untimely airing of information that unnecessarily inflamed the public. Contemporary wisdom dictates a list of media and other experts who can first form communications and public education strategies and then also respond during a crisis by communicating through many different mediums.

• *Incorporating Wisdom into the Planning Process.* Planning was not conducted as a part of a larger context within crisis management and the nuclear industry, and as a result, Three Mile Island failed to incorporate the lessons of many previous nuclear issues, including the experience of its own plant designer in a very similar issue just two years before.

The cornerstone lesson of Three Mile Island is the need to not only anticipate but to also plan for a weapons of mass destruction crisis. A holistic approach must provide planning, not as a linear process with mechanical parts, but rather as a social construct that interacts with the communities it is designed to protect. An unintegrated response will quickly turn mere failure into tragedy. It will take time to think through; it will take time to train to new standards; it will take time to practice. If a comprehensive approach is not taken, then not much good will have come from Three Mile Island, with the NRC's emergency response deputy director admitting as much:

Only if we exercise, get more and more people involved, will we make it work. The danger is that in a real emergency everyone will revert to instinct – and we will be right back to pre-Three Mile Island days.[346]

Response

The lack of crisis planning prior to Three Mile Island led to many of the response problems. Similarly for weapons of mass destruction response, an independent homeland security task force warns: "America's own ill-prepared response could hurt its people to a much greater extent than any single attack by a terrorist." Both systems lack(ed) the ability to respond to abstraction, which in the case of Three Mile Island was its radiation and its inevitable consequence - evacuation.

Radiation. Three Mile Island's first concern was radiation: What could be done? What were the possible effects? The plant itself had a critical shortage on protective gear (just as today's cities and counties possess critically low weapons of mass destruction protective supplies and equipment).[347]   Without supplies, the ability to respond was almost minimal once the release occurred. The best solution, therefore, was evacuation.

Even then, though, questions remain. At Three Mile Island, how might the effects of those who would have been exposed be alleviated? This question surfaced the importance of potassium iodide and forced an ad hoc response. Another knee jerk reaction was the belayed order and delivery of 70 tons of lead bricks to provide for additional plant containment.[348] Both measures suggest the need for well thought out surge capacities of various antidotes and physical requirements.

The second worry of radiation came from citizens: "how will the radiation affect me?" Time and systematic study would eventually prove negligible short- and long-term effects of the radiation release. The maximum exposure was approximately 85 millirems of radiation - the equivalent of two chest x-rays.[349] But people did not know this at the time, and without the facts, they made up their own. The most significant concern, therefore, was the psychological effects, which tied directly into the ensuingly chaotic evacuation.

Evacuations Are Hard. "Evacuation" is a difficult word to implement, possessed as it is with important conceptual and practical considerations. In any precarious situation, the last thing on the mind of a leader is anything that will make a situation less stable, especially in the absence of good information. Such was the case with Governor Thornburgh. The last thing he wanted was a "show of helmets" - anything that would increase fear and the sense of emergency while indicating that no one really knew what was going on.[350] Given the presence of so much faulty information, it is remarkable that Thornburgh did not overreact. His promulgation of an advisory (requesting the voluntary withdrawal of only a very small part of the population) teaches much about these types of situations.

The Governor's diction suggests that if one is creative enough, there is no need to be forced into an all-or-nothing decision. The advisory proved that when a well respected government official speaks, people listen. In a survey taken by Donald J. Ziegler, 53% of the population within 12 miles of Three Mile Island evacuated, while only 9% of those outside of 12 miles did so. 94% of those who evacuated, did so for "personal safety." Those who stayed did so because no specific order was given to evacuate, even though conflicting reports made people unsure (which was the second-most reason for leaving).[351] Also among these statistics is the point that the older the head of the household, the less likely the family evacuated.[352] Accurate demography will always factor in evacuations.

Evacuations reveal a "shadow phenomenon." If only the groups specifically addressed by the Governor had evacuated - women and pre-school children within five miles of the plant - then only 2,500 people would have left. Yet an estimated 144,000 people left.[353] When planning for an evacuation, the shadow phenomenon must be accounted for, particularly when the public perceives conflicting government information as part of the crisis.

Once it was officially "OK" to return, 54% of evacuees came back within four days.[354] Again, once the unknown was "made known" by an official announcement, most people trusted the announcement. The fear of the unknown will always drive behavior, and this simple observation of human nature is not one to be trivialized. Trust is the heart of an evacuation. It was only natural that people wanted to be safe. In this sense, evacuating was the ultimate coping mechanism.[355] The paradox of evacuating from radiation, however, is that "to get away from it, people have to go out into the very thing they're afraid of."[356] It could have been a lose-lose situation.

Recovery

The year after the crisis was spent scrubbing and cleaning. Physical clean-up was generally limited to the site itself, to include removal of the damaged fuel. The removal generated another consequence to be managed: the safe transport of the damaged fuel to an alternative storage facility.

Three Mile Island's recovery was conducted as poorly as the crisis response. Highlighted by delays, poor planning, and incompetence, it was marred by worker contamination during the cleanup. They stepped repeatedly in radioactive puddles, cleaned in unsafe conditions, and spilled radioactive materials. The most visible mistake was a shipment of radioactive material to the local incinerator for burning. The cleanup officially tallied ten workers with sustained high radiation readings, but many others most likely went unreported.

The economic costs were real but brief. Given the potential, $1 billion in cleanup was minimal. The voluntary evacuation resulted in a manufacturing loss of $7.7 million, and a non-manufacturing loss of $74 million. The vast majority of firms were back to normal by June.[357] Local legal claims (mostly for the amount of lost small business) were settled for $25 million.[358] Likewise, the public and mental health costs were settled for a small amount. The 280 claims for alleged emotional distress and radiation injuries settled for $3.9 million.[359]

These small claims are not unimportant as they remind of what the literal cost could have been. The Deputy Federal Insurance Administrator acknowledged at the time that if there had been a significant release, the estimated property damage would have been between $3-17 billion.[360] And that was just the property damage. A sufficient legal and financial framework for consequence management is perhaps the most mundane lesson, but in the end, the most relevant one for the afflicted. It is a tough framework to build, as one of Pennsylvania's insurance commission executives recognized:

We're dealing with the unknown. How do you assess damages for what may happen 20 years from now? The catastrophic potential is unknown...We can't see, hear, smell or taste radiation. How can we assess what damage might occur to farmland or human life?[361]

Interagency and Intergovernmental Relations

Three Mile Island involved no less than twenty-six agencies and their respective managers and leaders, all of whom attempted to resolve the crisis. While they clearly did not anticipate a nuclear problem, they were also not structured to respond to one in the tradition of federalism. The same issue that led to a reorganization of the post-Three Mile Island nuclear oversight process applies in many complex systems today, as evidenced by crisis management expert, Ian Mitroff:

What is required is a fundamental redesign of our agencies. Most of them were designed in and for far simpler times. They cannot cope with the complex systems that have evolved and that can easily elude the protections that might have been adequate in earlier times.[362]

When dealing with complex systems, one of government's fundamental issues is oversight, whether that oversight be in the United States or by other governments abroad. In the U.S. Constitutional framework, government oversight is one of the trickiest challenges; in complex systems it must be properly and appropriately considered. The bottom line is that high reliability systems have scrupulously sound oversight.

At Three Mile Island the NRC was responsible for regulation. The NRC knew the crisis had surpassed the plant operators' capabilities, yet it had no capability to take over the operation. A commonly perceived view of the NRC's lack of capabilities was expressed by a science reporter: "It's a dinky little backwater asshole agency that will drop back into obscurity when this is all over."[363]

The NRC never did drop back into obscurity. In the spotlight, it has still not corrected deficiencies that could hinder the management of weapons of mass destruction terrorism. A North Carolina waste reduction director, Jim Warren, says that the NRC "has consistently, over many years, gone along with what the nuclear industry has wanted to do," which creates "an extremely dangerous situation."[364] The NRC's manager of operations safety, Captain David Orrik, says:

Here it's the NRC-industrial complex. A lot of our upper management and commissioners have gone on to jobs in the nuclear industry. And I think some of them are much more attuned to he health and feeding of the industry than they are to public health and welfare.[365]

While the NRC must addresses these problems and provide sound oversight, homeland security analysts also value the contributions of industry in oversight, such as using private experts to simulate weapons of mass destruction threats and conduct government-sponsored assessments.[366] The great oversight challenge for weapons of mass destruction is the span of its control well beyond issues nuclear.

Moving down the scale from oversight to practical interagency operations, Three Mile Island offers lessons as well:

- *Local Government Coordination.* After the first morning, there was no contact from the power plant to the local county office of emergency preparedness (that would evacuate citizens). The governor's office never called the emergency managers either.
- *Incident Command.* Contrary to sound governmental crisis decision making, an incident command decision making structure was not followed during the crisis. During the wastewater release portion of the crisis, plant operators sought Bureau of Radiological Protection permission to release 400,000 gallons of wastewater into the Susquehanna River - and they did - but the Governor and the NRC did not know and the decision was ultimately reversed by the NRC. There was no clear chain of command for rapid decision making.
- *Interagency Communications.* There was talk among the key leaders and players, but there was no integrated response that connected federal, state, and local assets together. If there had been any true consequences to manage, the affect would have been devastating. Today, a very same lack of interagency communications plagues weapons of

mass destruction preparedness, with various fire, police, nuclear response, emergency medical, and military units using radio and information systems that cannot communicate with one another, lacking backup systems for redundancy, and possessing insecure communications systems.[367] Also missing are timely, accurate, and sharable incident tracking systems for public health threats.[368]

• *Interagency Participation Framework.* There was no attempt to link the various crisis centers at the federal, state, local, and private levels. Babcock & Wilcox could not get their team's analysis - that there was no oxygen in the reactor - to anyone who would listen. Met Ed's announcement that the bubble had disappeared fell on deaf ears, largely because it had no ears to fall on. PEMA came up with its own evacuation plans during the crisis. And while the local counties nominally had evacuation plans for a 5-mile radius, they were merely pieces of paper. They had never been rehearsed or coordinated with the other local counties, nor had the communities coordinated their plans with other levels of government. The one framework with the ability to organize and deploy in a coordinated manner to the scene of the accident was provided by the private sector. Initiated by GPU President Herman Dieckman, the Industry Advisory Group/Three Mile Island Recovery Group eventually included over 800 experts. Their sustained purpose was to: 1) maintain the current plant in a safe condition; 2) contain the release of radioactivity; and 3) make a reliable safe transition.[369] Such a group organized beforehand will significantly augment any consequence management effort today.

It Comes Down to People

Principles behind Three Mile Island's crisis have been repeated in other industries with completely different technologies. Some of these principles include: (1) leadership not wanting to hear bad news; (2) the "magic bullet" perception of new technology that does good with no harm; (3) old and new technologies and management systems creating a greater margin of error in their "transaction costs"; (4) extrapolation of smaller projects onto larger ones; and (5) failure to provide for redundant systems or providing redundant systems that are not truly redundant in that they interact with one another and a failure in one ripples into the other. The father of modern crisis management, Dr. Ian Mitroff observes as much:

In every crisis that I have ever studied, there have always been a few key people on the inside of an organization and on its edge who saw the early warning signs of imminent danger and tried desperately to warn their superiors. In every case, the signals were either ignored or blocked from getting to the top or having any effect. These signals were blocked not only by those internal to the organization but also by those external oversight agencies that should have been looking out for the interests of all concerned with the organization.[370]

Another student of the world's major historical crises, Eric Scigliano notes:

Though technologies change, many of the factors that make them go spectacularly wrong are surprisingly consistent: impatient clients who won't hear 'no'; shady or lazy designers who cut corners; excess confidence in glamorous new technologies; and, of course, good old-fashioned hubris.[371]

It is time to recognize that "the next Three Mile Island" does not have to be. Humans operating in complex systems can and should do what is required to oversee, manage, react, and recover for and from the contingencies they avoid and/or face. When crises do occur, they are not a result of society, technology, or science; they are a result of a person, persons, or entire industry or community not doing what they were supposed to do in order to appropriately design or manage the preparation and response of a complex system.

END NOTES

¹ This quotation is one of the Jefferson Memorial's ten chamber inscriptions chosen by the Thomas Jefferson Memorial Commission as being "most reflective of Jefferson's thought."

² Michael Hillyard, "What about your Block? A New Federal Department Is Much Needed...But the Fight Against Terror Begins Locally," *Newsday*, Opinion, November 24, 2002.

³ The full reference for the article is: Michael Hillyard, "Organizing for Homeland Security," *Parameters*, Spring 2002, 75-85.

⁴ James C. Collins and Jerry I. Porras, *Built to Last: Successful Habits of Visionary Companies* (New York: HarperCollins, 1994).

⁵ James Q. Wilson, *Bureaucracy: What Government Agencies Do and Why They Do It* (New York: Basic Books, 1989).

⁶ The White House, *President Establishes Office of Homeland Security*, Press Release, October 8, 2001.

⁷ The White House, *President Establishes Office of Homeland Security*, Press Release, October 8, 2001.

⁸ Douglas Waller, "A Toothless Tiger?," *Time*, October 15, 2001, 78.

⁹ Michael Elliott, "A Clear and Present Danger," *Time*, October 8, 2001, 37.

¹⁰ Elliott, 37.

¹¹ Advisory Panel to Assess Domestic Response Capabilities for Terrorism Involving Weapons of Mass Destruction, *Toward a National Strategy for Combating Terrorism*, December 15, 2000, ii.

[12] Michael J. Hillyard, *Public Crisis Management: How and Why Organizations Work Together to Solve Society's Most Threatening Problems* (Lincoln: Writers Club, 2000).

[13] The White House, *President Establishes Office of Homeland Security*, Press Release, October 8, 2001.

[14] The White House, *President Establishes Office of Homeland Security*, Press Release, October 8, 2001.

[15] Barry McCaffrey, "Challenges to US National Security," *Armed Forces Journal*, October 2001, 6.

[16] Advisory Panel to Assess Domestic Response Capabilities for Terrorism Involving Weapons of Mass Destruction, *Toward a National Strategy for Combating Terrorism*, December 15, 2000.

[17] McCaffrey, 8.

[18] Advisory Panel to Assess Domestic Response Capabilities for Terrorism Involving Weapons of Mass Destruction, *Toward a National Strategy for Combating Terrorism*, December 15, 2000, v.

[19] The Commission on US National Security/21st Century identified emergency management infrastructure as a potential homeland security asset. Such infrastructure, if implemented under the plan presented in this paper, would naturally fit into homeland security since most federal emergency management functions would fall under the aegis of the Department of Homeland Security. At the regional level, such alignment will also have to be realized.

[20] The full reference for the article is: Michael Hillyard, "Joint Military Principles in Homeland Security," *21st Century Defense: U.S. Joint Command*, Spring 2002, 48-55.

[21] Thucydides, *The Peloponnesian War*, 1,1,84,4. The quotation was observed by the author in Josiah Bunting III's, *An Education for Our Time* (Washington, D.C.: Regnery Publishing, 1998).

[22] *Second Annual Report of the Advisory Panel to Assess Domestic Response Capabilities for Terrorism Involving Weapons of Mass Destruction: Toward a National Strategy for Combating Terrorism,* December 15, 2000.

[23] The structure for homeland security is not the focus of this article, but readers may find the author's views in how to structure for homeland security in "Organizing for Homeland Security," *Parameters: U.S. Army War College Quarterly,* Volume 32, No. 1.

[24] *Second Annual Report of the Advisory Panel to Assess Domestic Response Capabilities for Terrorism Involving Weapons of Mass Destruction: Toward a National Strategy for Combating Terrorism,* December 15, 2000, iv.

[25] Chris Seiple, "The New Protracted Conflict: Homeland Security Concepts and Strategy," *Orbis,* Spring 2002, 259-260.

[26] Richard Falkenrath, "Problems of Preparedness: U.S. Readiness for a Domestic Terrorist Attack," *International Security,* 25.4. 2001, 174.

[27] "Joint Professional Military Education (JPME) is a collection of joint learning objectives that comprise the educational requirement for an officer to earn a Joint Specialty Officer (JSO) designation. JPME is usually divided into two phases: JPME Phase I consists of those joint learning objectives identified in the Chairman of the Joint Chiefs of Staff Officer Professional Military Education Policy (OPMEP) that are required to be included in intermediate and advanced service college's curriculum; JPME Phase II consists of those joint learning objectives contained in the intermediate and advanced courses offered by the Joint Forces Staff College. Officers who attend the

National War College or the Industrial College of the Armed Forces receive complete JPME credit." The preceding passage was taken from the US Naval War College's web site at http://pje.nps.navy.mil/faq.htm.

[28] Guy Oakes, *The Imaginary War: Civil Defense and American Cold War Culture* (New York: Oxford University Press, 1994), 167. The second set of quotations is referenced from Gary Ostrower's book review of Oakes's book, which can be found in *Historian*, 1994, Volume 59, Issue 1, 152-3.

[29] Kenneth Slepyan, "The Limits of Mobilisation: Party, State, and the 1927 Civil Defence Campaign," *Europe-Asia Studies*, 1993, Volume 45, Issue 5, 851-868.

[30] Kevin Johnson, "In the Heartland, a Call to Mobilize," *USA Today*, March 25, 2002, A1.

[31] In Seiple (p. 259), Robert Gates, "The Job Nobody Trained For," *The New York Times*, November 19, 2001.

[33] Johnson, A1.

[34] Cynthia Ramsay Taylor, Building Disaster-Resistant Communities, *USA Today Magazine (Life in America Section)*, July 2001, Volume 130, Issue 2674, 32.

[35] Johnson, A1.

[36] Gary Sheftick, "Homeland Security New Focus at War College," *ArmyLINK News Story*, 20 March 2002, 2.

[37] Johnson, A1.

[38] For more on Kennedy's civil service vision see Mark Huddleston and William Boyer, *The Higher Civil Service and the Quest for Reform* (Pittsburgh: University of Pittsburgh Press, 1996).

[39] The idea for foreign language education as a national security interest was discovered by the author

in Peter Schweizer, "Foreign Legion Could Answer USA's Military Needs," *USA Today*, March 25, 2002, A15.

[40] Johnson, A1.

[41] *Second Annual Report of the Advisory Panel to Assess Domestic Response Capabilities for Terrorism Involving Weapons of Mass Destruction: Toward a National Strategy for Combating Terrorism*, December 15, 2000.

[42] Falkenrath, 174.

[43] Thucydides, 1,1,84,4; in Bunting III.

[44] Johnson, A1.

[45] The Guard's institutional tensions have been raised by others, to include former Assistant Secretary of Defense for Reserve Affairs, Stephen Duncan in *Citizen Warriors: America's National Guard and Reserve Forces and the Politics of National Security* (Novato, CA: Presidio Press, 1997), xi.

[46] 481 times to be exact; see John Mahon, *History of the Militia and the National Guard* (New York: Simon and Schuster, 1983), 110.

[47] National Guard Bureau, "National Guard History," www.ngb.dtic.mil/about_us/ng_hst.shtml., April 3, 2002, 1.

[48] Dave Moniz, "'Ghost Soldiers Inflate Guard Numbers," *USA Today*, December 18, 2001, 1.

[49] Mahon, 128.

[50] Jim Drinkard, "National Guard Has Formidable Lobbying Power," *USA Today*, December 17, 2001, 2.

[51] Drinkard, 2.

[52] Mahon, 112.

[53] E. Colby, "Elihu Root and the National Guard," *Military Affairs*, Volume XXIII, No. 1, 1958, 30.

[54] Mahon, 120.

[55] Mahon, 238.

[56] Mahon, 232.

[57] Mahon, 265.

[58] United States General Accounting Office, *Report to the Subcommittee on National Security, Veteran's Affairs and International Relations, Committee on Government Reform, House of Representatives, Army National Guard: Enhanced Brigade Readiness Improved but Personnel and Workload Are Problems,* GAO/NSIAD-00-114, June 14, 2000.

[59] E. Philbin and J. Gould, "The Guard and Reserve: In Pursuit of Full Integration." In Bennie Wilson, ed., *The Guard and Reserve in the Total Force*, National Defense University, 1985.

[60] Arizona National Guard, *Soldier Support Handbook*, www.ngb.dtic.mil, April 3, 2002.

[61] Gary Hart and Warren Rudman (Co-Chairmen), *America Still Unprepared - America Still in Danger: Report of an Independent Task Force Sponsored by the Council on Foreign Relations* (New York: Council on Foreign Relations, 2002).

[62] United States General Accounting Office, *Report to the Subcommittee on National Security, Veteran's Affairs and International Relations, Committee on Government Reform, House of Representatives, Army National Guard: Enhanced Brigade Readiness Improved but Personnel and Workload Are Problems,* GAO/NSIAD-00-114, June 14, 2000.

[63] Duncan, 155.

[64] Moniz, 2.

[65] United States General Accounting Office, *Report to the Subcommittee on National Security, Veteran's Affairs and International Relations, Committee on Government Reform, House of Representatives, Army National Guard: Enhanced Brigade Readiness*

Improved but Personnel and Workload Are Problems, GAO/NSIAD-00-114, June 14, 2000.

[66] United States General Accounting Office, 4.

[67] United States General Accounting Office, 10.

[68] United States General Accounting Office, 17.

[69] National Guard Association, 1.

[70] Moniz and Drinkard.

[71] Dave Moniz and Jim Drinkard, "Four More Guard Leaders Probed," *USA Today*, April 4, 2002.

[72] Moniz, 8.

[73] Drinkard, 3.

[74] Richard Falkenrath, "Problems of Preparedness: U.S. Readiness for a Domestic Terrorist Attack," *International Security*, 25.4, 2001, 161.

[75] Graham, A01.

[76] Stanley Freedberg, "Pentagon Juggles Politics of Creating North American Command," *National Journal*, March 22, 2002.

[77] See Mahon.

[78] U.S. Commission on National Security, 6.

[79] U.S. Commission on National Security, 7.

[80] Donald Rumsfeld, "Transforming the Military," *Foreign Affairs*, May/June 2002, 23.

[81] Costa.

[82] Richard Falkenrath, Robert Neuman, and Bradley Thayer, *America's Achilles' Heel: Nuclear, Biological, and Chemical Terrorism and Covert Attack* (Cambridge, Massachusetts: The MIT Press, 1998), xxi.

[83] Falkenrath, 173.

[84] Falkenrath, 178.

[85] U.S. National Security Commission for the 21st Century, Phase III Report, 25-26.

[86] National Guard Association of the United States, "The Total Force Integration and Reserve Components

Equity Act of 1999," www.ngaus.org/legislative/ tie298.asp, 1.

[87] USC, Title 32, Chapter 1-Organization, Section 112.

[88] The Center for Law and the Public's Health at Georgetown and Johns Hopkins Universities, *The Model State Emergency Health Powers Act*, October 23, 2001.

[89] The Center for Law and the Public's Health at Georgetown and Johns Hopkins Universities, *The Model State Emergency Health Powers Act*, October 23, 2001.

[90] USC, Title 32, Chapter 1-Organization, Section 105.

[91] Zac Northrup, "The Fog of Washington," *National Guard Review*, Fall 1997.

[92] Bradley Graham, "Pentagon Wants Added Command," *The Washington Post*, January 26, 2002, A01.

[93] Freedberg.

[94] Joseph Barbara, et al., *Large-Scale Quarantine Following Biological Terrorism in the United States, Journal of the American Medical Association*, Volume 286, Number 21, 2712.

[95] Falkenrath, 182.

[96] Linda Kozaryn, "Bush Calls for 'Heartland' Security," *Armed Forces Press Service*, March 28, 2002.

[97] Linda Kozaryn, "Bush Calls for 'Heartland' Security," *Armed Forces Press Service*, March 28, 2002.

[98] Budget request amounts provided in Intellibridge Corporation, "Bush Seeking $50 Million for Citizen Corps," *Homeland Security Monitor*, April 8, 2002.

[99] George W. Bush, *Securing the Homeland, Strengthening the Nation*, Unpublished, 2002, 24.

[100] Bush, 24.

[101] Charles Moskos and Paul Glastries, "This Time, A Draft for the Home Front, Too," *The Washington Post*, November 4, 2001, B1.

[102] Duncan, 12.

[103] Bush, 2-6.

[104] In Duncan, 140.

[105] General Accounting Office, *Combating Terrorism: Use of National Guard Response Teams is Unclear, Testimony Before the Subcommittee on National Security, Veterans' Affairs, and International Relations, Committee on Government Reform, House of Representatives*, June 23, 1999.

[106] Drinkard, 2.

[107] Nancy O'Keefe Bolick, *Mail Call: The History of the U.S. Postal Service* (New York: Franklin Watts, 1994), 7.

[108] White House Press Release, www.whitehouse.gov/news/releases/2002/01/20020130-1.html, "President Creates USA Freedom Corps, January 31, 2002.

[109] *USA Freedom Corps Policy Book*, 5.

[110] Wayne Fuller, *The American Mail: Enlarger of the Common Life* (Chicago: University of Chicago Press, 1972).

[111] Culllinan, viii.

[112] Culllinan, viii.

[113] Fuller, 2.

[114] Fuller, 2.

[115] Roger Simon, et al. "Anthrax Nation," *U.S. News and World Report*, Volume 131, Issue 19, November 5, 2001, 14.

[116] Cullinan, 199.

[117] Carl Scheele, *A Short History of the Mail Service* (Washington: Smithsonian, 1970), 11.

[118] Scheele, 18.

[119] Scheele, 15.

[120] Scheele, 27.

[121] Bolick, 18.

[122] Cheryl Weant McAfee, *The United States Postal Service* (New York: Chelsea House, 1987), 17.

[123] Runyon.

[124] Bolick, 18.

[125] McAfee, 27.

[126] Time-Life, 27.

[127] Bolick, 38.

[128] The Editors of Time-Life Books with Text by David Nevin, *The Expressmen* (New York: Time, 1974), 7.

[129] McAfee, 32.

[130] Time-Life, 7.

[131] Time-Life, 23.

[132] Richard White, *A New History of the American West* (Norman: University of Oklahoma Press, 1991), 128.

[133] Noel Loomis, *Wells Fargo* (New York: Clarkson Potter, 1968), 171.

[134] Cullinan, 196.

[135] Cullinan, 197.

[136] Cullinan, 197.

[137] Scheele, 148.

[138] U.S. Post Office Department, *Annual Report 1942*, in Scheele, 173.

[139] Gerald Cullinan, *The United States Postal Service* (New York: Praeger, 1973), vii.

[140] Time-Life, 7.

[141] David Brin, *The Postman* (New York: Bantam Books, 1985), 50.

[142] Time-Life, 32.

[143] Cullinan, 130.

[144] Fuller.

[145] R. Conrad Stein, *The Story of the Pony Express* (Chicago: Regensteiner Publishing, 1981), 17.

[146] Stein, 20.

[147] Stein, 18.

[148] Time-Life, 30.

[149] Time-Life, 39.

[150] McAfee, 53.

[151] Stein, 27.

[152] Runyon.

[153] National Association of Letter Carriers, "We Deliver!" www.nalc.org/postal/wedelivr, January 28, 2002.

[154] National Association of Letter Carriers, "Half a Century of Help," October 10, 2001, www.nalc.org/commun/mda/index.html.

[155] Paul Carlin, "What the Future Holds for the U.S. Postal Service," *Vital Speeches of the Day*, Volume 61, Issue 17, June 15, 1995, 528.

[156] Loomis.

[157] Carlin.

[158] Unattributed, "One Woe After Another," *Economist*, Volume 361, Issue 8245, October 27, 2001, 30.

[159] *USA Freedom Corps Policy Book*, 4.

[160] U.S. Postal Inspection Service, "How to Protect Your Mail from Thieves," www.usps.com/postalinspectors/tipthief.htm, 2.

[161] National Association of Letter Carriers, "NALC's Carrier Alert Program," www.nalc.org/commun/alert/index.html, October 10, 2001.

[162] National Association of Letter Carriers, "NALC's Carrier Alert Program," www.nalc.org/commun/alert/index.html, October 10, 2001.

[163] National Association of Letter Carriers, "NALC's Carrier Alert Program," www.nalc.org/commun/alert/index.html, October 10, 2001.

[164] George Bush, *Security the Homeland, Strengthening the Nation*, Unpublished, 2002.

[165] Bush.

[166] *USA Freedom Corps Policy Book*, 5.

[167] Runyon.

[168] Runyon.

[169] Fuller, 264.

[170] Tom Bethell, "With Enough Shovels," *American Spectator*, Volume 35, Issue 1, 78.

[171] Waring.

[172] Waring.

[173] Waring.

[174] U.S. Postal Inspection Service, "How to Protect Your Mail from Thieves," www.usps.com/postalinspectors/tipthief.htm, 2.

[175] Dean Foust and Gerry Khermouch, "A Hit to the Mail is a Hit to the Economy," *Business Week*, Issue 3758, 40.

[176] Unattributed, "Mr. ZIP Goes to War," *Kiplinger's Personal Finance*, May 2002, Volume 56, Issue 5, 21.

[177] McAfee, 18.

[178] McAfee, 22.

[179] McAfee, 37.

[180] McAfee, 46.

[181] Runyon.

[182] McAfee.

[183] Paula Cole, *Where Have All the Cowboys Gone*, CD-Single, May 21, 1997.

[184] National and Voluntary Service are categorized in the following article: Unattributed, "A Nation of Volunteers," *The Economist*, Volume 362, Issue 8261, February 23, 2002, 40.

[185] George Bush, Address to the Citizens of the United States, September 12, 2001.

[186] Kevin Johnson, "In the Heartland, A Call to Mobilize," *USA Today*, March 25, 2002, 2A.

[187] U.S. Commission on National Security for the 21st Century, Executive Summary.

[188] Office of Homeland Security, *National Strategy for Homeland Security*, Washington, D.C., July 16, 2002, vii.

[189] Harris Wofford, "Promoting Intergenerational Strategies: The Role of the Corporation for National Service," *Generations*, Winter 98/99, Volume 22, Issue 4, 88.

[190] Richard Falkenrath, et al., *America's Achilles Heel: Nuclear, Biological, and Chemical Terrorism and Covert Attack* (Cambridge: The MIT Press, 1998), 280.

[191] George Bush, in Office of Homeland Security, *National Strategy for Homeland Security*, Washington, D.C., July 16, 2002, iii.

[192] In Guy Oakes's, *The Imaginary War: Civil Defense and American Cold War Culture* (New York: Oxford University Press, 1994).

[193] Michael Dobbs, "A Renaissance for U.S. Civil Defense?," *Journal of Homeland Security*, July 2001.

[194] Tom Kenworthy, "U.S. Fire Policy Isn't Cutting It," *USA Today*, http://www.usatoday.com/news/nation/2002-08-21-1acover_x.htm, August 22, 2002.

[195] Kenworthy.

[196] U.S. General Accounting Office, *Combating Terrorism: Critical Components of a National Strategy to Enhance State and Local Preparedness*, GAO-02-548T, March 25, 2002, 9.

[197] The Office of Homeland Security and the Homeland Security Council, "President Establishes Office of Homeland Security," Press Release, October

8, 2001, www.whitehouse.gov/news/releases/2001/10/ 2001'1008.html.

[198] Carlson.

[199] Falkenrath, et al. 7.

[200] Chris Seiple, Interview with author, September 2, 2002.

[201] USA Freedom Corps, National Crime Prevention Council, and U.S. Department of Justice, *United for a Stronger America: Citizens' Preparedness Guide* (Washington, D.C.: National Crime Prevention Council, 2002).

[202] Severyn Bruyn, "Solution: Civilian-Based Defense," *Futurist*, January/February 2002, Volume 36, Issue 1, 20; the first portion of this quotation was moved from the back of Bruyn's remarks to the front of this citation of them in order to more appropriately reflect the context in which they are being used.

[203] Charles Moskos and Paul Glastris, "This Time, A Draft for the Homefront, Too," *The Washington Post*, November 4, 2001, B1.

[204] Thomas Massaro, "Social Policy after Sept. 11," *Social Policy*, Volume 186, Issue 7, 16.

[205] Margaret Carlson, "All Together Now," *Time*, Volume 159, Issue 6, 33.

[206] Office of Homeland Security, *National Strategy for Homeland Security*, Washington, D.C., July 16, 2002, 2.

[207] Potachuk and Crocker, 175.

[208] William Vogele, "Deterrence by Civil Defense," *Peace and Change*, January 1993, Volume 18, Issue 1, 26.

[209] Dobbs.

[210] Jane Goodall, "The Power of One," *Time*, Volume 160, Number 9, August 26, 2002, A62.

[211] USA Freedom Corps, National Crime Prevention Council, and U.S. Department of Justice, *United for a Stronger America: Citizens' Preparedness Guide* (Washington, D.C.: National Crime Prevention Council, 2002).

[212] USA Freedom Corps, National Crime Prevention Council, and U.S. Department of Justice, *United for a Stronger America: Citizens' Preparedness Guide* (Washington, D.C.: National Crime Prevention Council, 2002).

[213] Kevin Johnson, "In the Heartland, A Call to Mobilize," *USA Today*, March 25, 2002, 2A.

[214] Dobbs.

[215] Dobbs.

[216] Cynthia Taylor Ramsey, "Building Disaster-Resistant Communities," *USA Today Magazine*, July 2001, Volume 130, Issue 2674, 32.

[217] Dobbs.

[218] Dobbs.

[219] The Kearney Commission.

[220] Staff Report to the President's Commission on the Accident at Three Mile Island, "Report of the Emergency Preparedness and Response Task Force," 27.

[221] Dobbs.

[222] Paul Maniscalco and Hank Christen, *Terrorism Response: Field Guide for Law Enforcement* (Upper Saddle River, New Jersey: Pearson Education, 2003), 11.

[223] Maniscalco and Christen, 18.

[224] Michael Hillyard, *Public Crisis Management: How and Why Organizations Work Together to Solve Society's Most Threatening Problems* (Lincoln: Writers Club, 2000), 20.

[225] Michael Kinsley, "How to Live a Rational Life," *Time*, September 9, 2002, 113.

[226] Andrew Sullivan, "Yes, America Has Changed," *Time*, September 9, 2002, 46.

[227] A central Pennsylvania T-shirt, Laurence Stern et al., "Tensions Ease as the Bubble is Chased Away," *The Washington Post*, April 11, 1979, A1.

[228] Potorti, 19.

[229] Charles Perrow, *Normal Accidents: Living with High-Risk Technologies* (Princeton: Princeton University Press, 1999).

[230] Stephens, 76.

[231] Rod Nordland, et al., "Where is the Next Chernobyl?" *Newsweek*, Volume 134, Issue 16, 34.

[232] Nordland, et al., 34.

[233] Scott Moore, "The Study of Disasters," *Social Science Journal*, Volume 38, Issue 1, 173.

[234] White, 26.

[235] Thomas White, "The Establishment of Blame in the Aftermath of a Technological Disaster," *National Forum*, Winter 2001, Volume 81, Issue 1, 24.

[236] White, 26.

[237] Stephens, 6.

[238] Stephens, 5.

[239] H. George Frederickson and Todd LaPorte, "Airport Security, High Reliability, and the Problem of Rationality," *Public Administration Review*, Volume 62, Special Issue.

[240] Anne D. Trunk and Edward V. Trunk, "Three Mile Island: A Resident's Perspective," in *The Three Mile Island Accident: Lessons and Implications*, ed. Thomas H. Moss and David L. Sills (New York: The New York Academy of Sciences, 1981), 179.

[241] Henry L. Hinton, Jr., Assistant Comptroller General, National Security and International Affairs

Division, General Accounting Office, Testimony Before the Subcommittee on National Security, Veterans' Affairs, and International Relations, Committee on Government Reform, House of Representatives, "Combating Terrorism: Observations on the Threat of Chemical and Biological Terrorism," October 20, 1999, 1.

[242] Gary Hart and Warren Rudman (Co-Chairmen), *America Still Unprepared - America Still in Danger: Report of an Independent Task Force Sponsored by the Council on Foreign Relations* (New York: Council on Foreign Relations, 2002), 5.

[243] Richard A. Falkenrath, et al. *America's Achilles' Heel* (Cambridge: The Belfer Center for Science and International Affairs, 1998), 214. Also, see James K Campbell, *Weapons of Mass Destruction and Terrorism: Proliferation by Non-State Actors* (Thesis for the Naval Postgraduate School, Monterey, California, December 1996); and Seth W. Carus, "Working Paper: Bioterrorism and Biocrimes," (Center for Counterproliferation Research, National Defense University, August 1998 (July 1999 Revision)).

[244] Richard Preston, in Anita Manning, "'Demon' Possesses Scary Bioterrorism News," *USA Today*, October 28, 2002, 7D.

[245] Bethell, 79.

[246] Hart and Rudman, 17.

[247] Paul Gunnessy, "Security at US Nuclear Power Plants Boosted after Terrorist Attacks," *Physics Today*, Volume 54, Issue 12, December 2001, 20.

[248] Mark Clayton, "Core Concerns," *Christian Science Monitor*, Volume 94, Issue 162, July 16, 2002, 11.

[249] Pasternak, 44.

[250] Pasternak, 44.

[251] Clayton, 11.

[252] Potorti, 18.

[253] David Potorti, "Nuclear Danger Zone, NC," *Nation*, Volume 273, Issue 1, 18.

[254] In Bethell, 78.

[255] Harvey Wasserman, "Nuclear Power and Terrorism," *Earth Island Journal*, Spring 2002, Volume 17, Issue 1, 37.

[256] Wasserman, 27.

[257] Bethell, 79.

[258] Bethell, 79.

[259] Unless otherwise noted, the following description is based on the two most thorough accounts of the accident: (1) The President's Commission on the Accident at Three Mile Island, "The Need for Change: The Legacy of Three Mile Island," October 1979, 110-161 [Hereafter cited as The Kemeny Commission.]; and (2) Nuclear Regulatory Commission, Special Inquiry Group, "Three Mile Island: A Report to the Commissioners and to the Public," January 1980, 1-87 [Hereafter cited as The Rogovin Report].

[260] Stephens, 12.

[261] Stephens, 12.

[262] The Rogovin Report, 20. It would later be determined that 70% of the core was damaged while 35-45% of it had actually melted. William Booth, "Postmortem on Three Mile Island," *Science*, December 4, 1987, 1342.

[263] Stephens, 34.

[264] Stephens, 47.

[265] Stephens, 33.

[266] Stephens, 48.

[267] Stephens, 51.

[268] Stephens, 41.

[269] Stephens, 100.

[270] The NRC press release and its effect based on The Rogovin Report, 48-51.

[271] Stephens, 58.

[272] Stephens, 60.

[273] Stephens, 163.

[274] Stephens, 169.

[275] As is so often the case in Washington, the White House involvement started with a "back-door" call from one of the NRC commissioners to a personal contact at the NSC (Jessica Tuchman Matthews). Matthews immediately informed her boss, National Security Advisor Zbigniew Brzezinski. Matthews remained the White House point-of-contact throughout, although the official lead was Jack Watson. Thornburgh was personally briefed by Matthews over the phone that Friday afternoon (The Rogovin Report, 70-71).

[276] Stephens, 191.

[277] All quotations as recorded in Raymond L. Goldsteen and John K. Schorr, *Demanding Democracy After Three Mile Island* (Gainesville: University of Florida Press, 1991), 27-29.

[278] Stephens, 130.

[279] Stephens, 131.

[280] Stephens, 134.

[281] Stephens, 160.

[282] Stephens, 164.

[283] Stephens, 162.

[284] Stephens, 41.

[285] IPC Productions, *The China Syndrome*, 1978.

[286] Stephens, 27-28.

[287] Stephens, 29.

[288] Stephens, 82.

[289] Stephens, 105.

[290] Richard Preston, in Anita Manning, "'Demon' Possesses Scary Bioterrorism News," *USA Today*, October 28, 2002, 7D.

[291] Stephens, 146.

[292] Stephens, 74.

[293] Stephens, 74.

[294] Stephens, 74.

[295] Stephens, 74.

[296] Stephens, 84.

[297] Thomas Shriver, et al., "The Role of Collective Identity in Inhibiting Mobilization: Solidarity and Suppression in Oak Ridge," *Sociological Spectrum*, Volume 20, Issue 1, January-March 2000, 41.

[298] Bob Davis, Dauphin County Mental Health Crisis Intervention Center, as quoted in Laurence Stern et al., "Tensions Ease as the Bubble is Chased Away," *The Washington Post*, April 11, 1979, A1.

[299] Stephens, 230.

[300] Evelyn Bromet and Leslie Dunn, "Mental Health of Mothers Nine Months After the Three Mile Island Accident," *The Urban and Social Change Review*, Summer 1981, 13-14.

[301] Hart and Rudman, 29.

[302] The Kemeny Commission, 17.

[303] As quoted in J.R. Wargo, "Three Mile Island: Now for the Answers," *Nuclear Industry*, May 1979, 5.

[304] Stephens, 188.

[305] Peter G. Stillman, "Three Mile Island: A Case of Disinformation," *Democracy*, Fall 1982, 67.

[306] J.R. Wargo, "Three Mile Island: Now for the Answers," 16.

[307] Peter Grier, "Got a Nuclear Crisis? Better Call NEST," *Christian Science Monitor*, Volume 92, Issue 148, June 22, 2000, 1.

308 Jeffrey Richelson, "Defusing Nuclear Terror," *Bulletin of the Atomic Scientists*, Volume 58, Issue 2, March/April 2002, 38.

309 Hart and Rudman, 34.

310 Laurence Stern et al., "A Presidential Tour to Calm Fears," *The Washington Post*, April 10, 1979, A1.

311 The Kemeny Commission, 140.

312 The Rogovin Report, 68.

313 Peter M. Sandman and Mary Paden, "At Three Mile Island," *Columbia Journalism Review*, July/August 1979, 50.

314 Stephens, 77.

315 Stephens, 77.

316 Also, by making Three Mile Island operational before the start of 1979, Met Ed saved $40 million in taxes (Laurence Stern et al., "Danger of Day Three: Nuclear Shower if the Core Melts," *The Washington Post*, April 9, 1979, A1.).

317 As quoted in Peter M. Sandman and Mary Paden, "At Three Mile Island," 47.

318 Sandman and Paden, "At Three Mile Island," 57.

319 Sharon M. Friedman, "Blueprint for Breakdown: Three Mile Island and the Media Before the Accident," *Journal of Communication*, Spring 1981, 122.

320 Stephens, 183.

321 Stephens, 15.

322 Stephens, 16.

323 IPC Productions, *The China Syndrome*, 1978.

324 Stephens, 117.

325 Clayton, 11.

326 Hart and Rudman, 21.

327 Thomas H. Pigford, "The Management of Nuclear Safety: A Review of Three Mile Island after Two Years," *Nuclear News*, March 1981, 42.

[328] Kriebel and Tickner, 1353.

[329] IPC Productions, *The China Syndrome*, 1978.

[330] Stephens, 27.

[331] Stephens, 30.

[332] Stephens, 152.

[333] Evelyn Bromet and Leslie Dunn, "Mental Health of Mothers Nine Months After the Three Mile Island Accident," *The Urban and Social Change Review*, Summer 1981, 14.

[334] Stephens, 196.

[335] Hart and Rudman, 31.

[336] David Kriebel and Joel Tickner, "Reenergizing Public Health Through Precaution," *American Journal of Public Health*, Volume 91, Issue 9, September 2001, 1351.

[337] Tom Bethell, "With Enough Shovels," *American Spectator*, Volume 35, Issue 1, Jan/Feb 2002, 78.

[338] Stephens, 231.

[339] Stephens, 56.

[340] Stephens, 48.

[341] The Kemeny Commission, 15-16. Also see the supporting report on "Emergency Preparedness, Emergency Response," 147. The Commission describes county and state officials planning evacuation routes and accounting for the transport of the incapacitated early in the morning of Saturday, March 31, 1979.

[342] Stephens, 116.

[343] Bethell, 78.

[344] Stephens, 136.

[345] Andrew P. Hull, "Emergency Preparedness for What? (Implications of the Three Mile Island - 2 Accident)," *Nuclear News*, April 1981, 66.

[346] Arlie Schardt, "Covering Three Mile Island," *Newsweek*, April 16, 1979, 93.

[347] Sheldon Schwartz, Deputy Director of the NRC's emergency preparedness division, as quoted in Orr Kelly, "Is U.S. Prepared for a New Three Mile Island?" *U.S. News & World Report*, March 19, 1984, 58.

[348] Hart and Rudman, 20.

[349] Laurence Stern et al., "Danger of Day Three: Nuclear Shower if the Core Melts," *The Washington Post*, April 9, 1979, A1.

[350] Cordell, "After Chernobyl: Where Do We Go From Here?" *USA Today*, November 1987, 50.

[351] The Rogovin Report, 86.

[352] Donald J. Ziegler, et al., "Evacuation from a Nuclear Technological Disaster," *The Geographical Review*, January 1981, 3-6.

[353] The Governor's Office of Policy and Planning, "The Socio-Economic Impacts of the Three Mile Island Accident," July 17, 1981, 1.

[354] Donald J. Ziegler, et al., "Evacuation from a Nuclear Technological Disaster," 7.

[355] Zeigler et al., 9.

[356] Zeigler et al., "Evacuation from a Nuclear Technological Disaster," 12.

[357] Dr. Glenn Bartlett of the Hershey Medical Center (located eight miles from Three Mile Island), as quoted in Sandra Edwards, "Three Mile Island's Worst Casualty: Stress," *Science Digest*, May 1980, 76.

[358] The Governor's Office of Policy and Planning, "The Socio-Economic Impacts of the Three Mile Island Accident," July 17, 1981, ii.

[359] Ben A. Franklin, "Agreement Reached in 3 Mile Island Suit," *The New York Times*, February 22, 1981, 1.

[360] William O. Doub and James R. Shoemaker, "Who Pays the Costs of Industrial Accidents Like Three Mile Island?" *Public Utilities Fortnightly*, May 16, 1985, 16.

[361] Larry Kramer, "Insurance Regulator Decries Nuclear Accident Coverage," *The Washington Post*, April 18, 1979, A10.

[362] As quoted in Elaine S. Knapp, "Fallout Begins from Atomic Accident," *State Government News*, May 1979, 8.

[363] Mitroff, 18.

[364] Stephens, 121.

[365] Potorti, 18.

[366] Potorti, 19.

[367] Hart and Rudman.

[368] Hart and Rudman, 10, 20.

[369] Hart and Rudman, 30.

[370] J.R. Wargo, "Three Mile Island: Now for the Answers," 16.

[371] Mitroff, 18.

[372] Eric Scigliano, "10 Technological Disasters," *Technology Review*, Volume 15, Issue 5, June 2002, 48.

LaVergne, TN USA
06 January 2010
169013LV00001B/56/A